She is

WITHOUT LIMITS

by

HALEY HOFFMAN SMITH

www.sheiswithoutlimits.com

Guidance & Editing by Kelly Hart.
Special thanks to Janet Lee Burnet.
Interior Layout by Country Mouse Designs.

ISBN: 978-0-692-82337-8

She is

ACKNOWLEDGING THOSE WHO MADE THIS POSSIBLE:

I could say that this book was a labor of love, but the truth is, it was all love.

Thank you to the women who have led the charge before me.

This book would not have been possible without the support and encouragement of some incredible individuals in my life.

Thank you, first and foremost, to the sensational Kelly Hart — how you have understood and valued me from Day One has led to unprecedented courage in sharing my voice and heart with the world. You have urged me onward when my voice wavered, reminded me of my purpose when I was distracted, and turned the small flame of a dream into a raging wildfire.

Thank you to my mother, for implementing these beliefs deeply in my being, and teaching me I am worthy of the best of everything that life must offer; and to my father, for encouraging me to find truth and ecstasy with pen and paper.

Thank you to each of my co-authors for believing in my vision and devoting your time, insight, and heart to make this project possible.

RS - Your devotion to academia in feminism and literature has had implications far outside the classroom — thank you for encouraging my formulation of my own ideals, and joining me in the "sisterhood of the traveling pen."

Thank you to every friend — old and new — who celebrated this venture with the utmost love, rushed to pre-order the book, and exalted girl power and sisterhood with me. Much of who I am is sustained in these sweet friendships.

To NPH - for seeing me perfectly and loving me perfectly. You are my wings.

CONTENTS

FOREWORD

TO EMPOWERED (AND YET-TO-BE-EMPOWERED) WOMEN EVERYWHERE:

I have found that many of us live with certain limitations, although we may not be fully aware of them. Some limits are imposed on us by social expectations and cultural pressures, but some we unknowingly place on ourselves. It is often said that the only thing standing in our way is ourselves. Perhaps the limits we create are the only thing preventing self-actualization and fulfillment.

It is not until we fully recognize our self-imposed limits that we may effectively eliminate them. I hope this book helps you see the immense value you bring to the world, and shows you how to tap into your full potential and live the happiest life possible. Bliss is our birthright, and authentic bliss bursts at our seams when we go deep within ourselves and serve others. You deserve this bliss. We all do.

I have written this book to encourage greater self-awareness in each reader. With the help of a gathering of remarkable women, you will discover, grow, enrich and shape your self-concept. We will heighten your self-understanding, and know that you can rise; that you are without limits.

I hope it resonates.

I hope it makes you think.

I hope it empowers you in courage, love, and service.

By beginning this book, you are beginning a journey to the ultimate self-love. Thank yourself for the desire to look within. Get real, get messy. Lean on the women in your circle, and know that you are supported - in heart, mind, body, and soul.

Here's to a girl without limits.

Haley Hoffman Smith

1

She is

CLAIMING HER POWER

WHEN I WAS A CHILD, I would position my stuffed animals in a circle on the rug in my room. I would stand by the wall, scribbling on my chalkboard, teaching them everything I had learned in school. They each had names — personalities from Omar the Orangutan (as named by my mother), to Teddy the Teddy Bear (named by myself), and they raised their hands to be called on as if they knew the answer to the many scholastic questions I would pose. I loved the hours spent pretending to be a teacher — treating each furry animal with the attention and respect I would have given to real students.

As it turned out, a decade later, I would find joy and fulfillment mentoring girls in middle school. I was able to share lessons and values I'd learned. I went on to find a similar love and passion in academia. The hours spent "pretending" as a small child ultimately held larger implications.

When we are children, and the limits of make-believe are

blurry, we experiment with being whoever we want to be. This is the time and space before we are susceptible to definitions of what is successful, what is respectable, and what is worthwhile to pursue. Essentially, our curiosities in childhood represent inherent authenticity. These curiosities stay with us long into adulthood, whether or not we pursue them.

Think back to your own early days. How you define yourself now (as BIG as that definition may be) is sprinkled with inclinations, interests, hobbies and habits that started when you were small. What I hope to remind you in the following chapters is the power you hold in just being YOU. You are an extraordinary individual, with traits so unique that no one else can duplicate them.

Even the greatest humans don't have every detail ironed out and every nail in place. They simply understand what they excel at, and what they shouldn't spend time on. When we exert our energy toward what naturally energizes us (hint: what we loved as children and continue to love now), our power multiplies and becomes greater than what we imagined.

In other words, *love* is power. And the greatest, warm and buzzy love is the love that propels us to devote time to something that serves others. This can be widely interpreted. Maybe you're an artist who loves experimenting with charcoal sketches. In some way, that's going to bring joy to someone who sees it. Maybe it's more explicit. Maybe you find yourself energized by community service, a direct way of impacting others. Or maybe you're the writer who writes for herself, in her room late at night with just a small light, knowing the words you pen are for your eyes solely. If your writing fuels the love and energy inside you, it is worthwhile. Trust in that.

I urge you to commit to a love so big that it becomes a power within itself. I urge you to commit to a love so big that it envelops all that you do. I urge you to act out of love in even the smallest of actions, even those you believe don't impact others, even those toward yourself – no, *especially* those toward yourself. This is the first and most critical step toward living without limits.

Write down: Your childhood hobbies / pastimes.

Write down: Your current hobbies / pastimes.

What do you LOVE to do? (the type of love that transcends time, keeps you engaged, makes your cheeks buzz with warmth.)

How does what you love to do serve? (Serve yourself, or serve others)

2

She is

CONFRONTING HER LIMITS

I'M NOT A MATH GIRL, but from the little I know of calculus, I understand there is a concept called "limits". The limit is defined as what a function nears as it approaches its value.

Now, I am certainly a word girl, and there are some words in this definition I can work with. What if calculus is onto something philosophical? What if, in order to truly understand our value (and come as close as possible to realizing our value), we need to get up-close-and-personal with our limits?

There are limits we encounter but don't recognize. There are also those we have noticed, but swept under the rug. Maybe they're socially imposed beliefs. Perhaps someone spoke to you cruelly, or an experience shifted how you view your capabilities. These things may echo in your mind, putting up roadblocks when you dare yourself to do something big or new. I'm here to say that it's okay. There is no need to be ashamed of these restraints. But we do want to recognize them, so that we may effectively eliminate them.

I can't speak to what may be limiting YOU as an individual, so I'm going to cover two challenges that many people struggle with every day. Maybe they don't apply to you. If not, congratulations! You're already ahead of the game. But maybe they do, whether you're comfortable admitting it or not, and this chapter will help you recognize that you have the ability to break through.

1. SOCIAL MEDIA / PHONE TIME

WAIT! Before you skip to #2 or Chapter 3, for that matter, let's get real for a moment. I could be the poster child for this topic. I use every social media you can imagine. I'd bring Myspace back, if I could, just to have another way to connect with everyone I've ever met. I get on the upper end of 200 texts a day (I wish this was an exaggeration), and at least 50 emails - to my four separate email accounts.

I am constantly tuned in and connected, and it's great in a lot of ways. I am legitimately energized by talking and networking with friends and acquaintances. Recently, I moved to Rhode Island from Colorado. Social media allows me to stay in touch with Colorado friends and family while checking out what my new Rhode Island friends are up to. It also allows me to connect with movers and shakers who are doing cool things and sharing cool songs and quotes.

But sometimes — for Pete's sake — I just have to disconnect! We all do.

This age has made it virtually impossible (ha!) to be truly alone. In some ways, this is a blessing: I feel as though I've brought my Colorado friends and family along to Rhode Island. But in other ways, it is a serious hindrance.

Time alone is critical. When we're truly alone, forced to listen to our thoughts or commit 100% of our attention to a task at hand, amazing things can happen. But sometimes, being alone can be uncomfortable. Sometimes unwelcome thoughts or emotions bubble to the surface. We can find strength in facing these unpleasantries, staring them down, and telling them to move along. We have the power to move through — and beyond — the loneliness, sadness, or worry. We can heal and become neutral to painful memories that return. What this requires is being totally present (more on this later).

Another element of social media that I need to mention is a tad cringeworthy. We live in an age where everything we do can be public, if we so please. I sometimes think about my parent's age — they only had the home phone, attached to the wall, and if they wanted to make a statement or prove a point, they had to say it directly to that person over the phone or face-to-face. Nowadays there are ample mediums for making a point, and not only that person but any number of friends can pick up on it. It gives breakups and fights an interesting new dynamic. If you want to prove, or pretend, that you're A-Okay after a breakup, it's as simple as a happy Instagram post or a raging Snapchat story. If there's something you want to say to a friend that you don't want to say directly, you can use a "subtweet" - just share your feelings publicly without even mentioning their name and they'll see it and get the point. They'll probably check your Twitter page, as you'll check theirs, and there will be this weird pseudo-communication for a second. This is a *serious limitation* to authenticity, communication, and happiness.

None of this is to say that I don't approve of social media. That would be hypocritical. But central to understanding our limits is recognizing the intentions behind what we do. For example - it is one thing to share a great picture of yourself because it's fun and you want to share the joy. But sharing a picture just to prove a point (or prove your worth), is entirely different. Social media can be used to cultivate others' perceptions of who we are and how our life is. Choose to be authentic instead. If you are grieving a breakup, stay off social media for a second. If you are celebrating an accomplishment — by all means, SHARE IT! If you want to share your new haircut, DO IT! But don't put energy into creating a false front for yourself. Don't do things solely to influence other people's perceptions of you. How you feel about yourself reigns supreme, and only a select few will ever have an accurate perception of who you are. They are your besties. They know you, heart and soul. You do not need to impress them. They already love you.

2. (WASN'T #1 MORE FUN THAN YOU THOUGHT?!) AND NOW, FOR YOUR EGO!

I didn't know I had an ego problem until I was crying in my mother's arms last December. Let me back up a bit. I was crying because aspects of my life (how I viewed myself and how I viewed others) were starting to crumble around me. I was desperate to prove myself. I needed to be the *best* at everything... at the cost of my relationships with dear friends, and even my brother. My impatience and self-indignance had gotten the best of me, and I finally realized how truly unhappy I was.

It is one thing to have self-love. It is another thing, entirely, to have *feigned* self-love. We should absolutely praise ourselves for our accomplishments. But things get messy when a person relies on accomplishments alone for their self-worth. My messy was pretty bad. And in that moment, I realized that even if we aren't explicitly ego-driven, there are behaviors I observe in myself (and others, too, at times) that represent ego.

First and foremost, what is ego? Ego is a person's sense of self-esteem or self-importance. Although most people think of ego in terms of how highly one thinks of one's self, the ego's primary function is to protect us. The ego is tasked with finding a balance between our primitive drive and the moral implications of playing out those desires. The ego's main concern is with the individual's safety. Issues with the ego typically show up in 1 of 2 ways: inflated self-esteem / self-centered living or low self-esteem / deflated self-worth.

Believing that you are better than others is an ego-driven belief. Love will tell you we are equal, but ego values external factors like the college you attend, the clothes you wear, your GPA, etc. The mere existence of ego leads to the judgment of others. It is our job to quiet the ego, look beneath the surface, and come from love.

I've generally been more critical of others when I, myself, feel insecure. Again, the ego protects, and tries to reassure us by focusing on other people's faults. If you find yourself judging others, take a step back. Is it rooted in your own insecurity? If you feel insecure, where is it coming from? Can it be worked on? Take control over what you can change. Disregard what you cannot.

Remember that your value and self-image is decided by you alone.

Another way ego shows up is through jealousy or envy, which actually clue us into what we *truly want* for ourselves. It's worth noting that you never know what anyone else is dealing with behind closed doors. The seemingly "perfect" kid at school might be struggling with an alcoholic parent at home. The Homecoming Queen may be battling depression or severe anxiety. Try not to make assumptions about how someone else's life is. Focus on what *you* truly want and being the best *you* can be. Find comfort in your own shoes and extend kindness to everyone.

Ego can also be identified as a constant need for more. You may think you need more money, more stuff, better grades, more accolades. Where is the desire coming from? Are you trying to fill a void? When you feel love, and more importantly, have self-love, you don't need more. Shifting to a love mindset allows you to find joy in the present moment and peace within yourself.

So, as I was falling apart in my mom's arms, realizing how devoid my heart was of love for myself (and others), she gave me a bit of advice. She told me to construct a new sense of self — grounded in love, absent of ego. She suggested I start doing things for others, completely anonymously. As I thought this advice over, a sense of patience and stillness came over me.

My tone became kinder.

I became more present.

I valued what others said.

I began to slow down and act with love. I analyzed different areas of my life to learn where I was acting from ego. Becoming conscious of the way our ego rules our lives is the first step toward eliminating its hold on us. It is no small task. The more aware we become of our shortcomings and how they affect us and others, the more opportunities we have to grow. Once we tune in, we can take control.

HOW TO IDENTIFY EGO-DRIVEN BEHAVIORS:

1. Do you seek approval from others, or need validation from social media?

2. Do you compare yourself to others, or judge them on superficial qualities?

3. Are you competitive or feel the need to always be right?

4. Do you ever feel fully satisfied? Or do you constantly need *more?*

5. Are you able to be fully present, without checking your phone or checking the clock?

6. Are you willing to ask for help when you need it?

HOW TO REPLACE EGO-DRIVEN BEHAVIORS WITH LOVE-BASED ONES:

1. Abandon your pride.

2. Let go of the constant need to assert yourself.

3. Seek to understand others more deeply.

4. Focus on the best in people.

5. Accept and embrace individual differences.

6. Truly see everyone as equal.

Understand that you have *power* over your experience. Love yourself enough to eliminate toxic habits and ego-driven behaviors. Recognize that the present is all you have, and time is one of your greatest gifts. Once you clear yourself of limiting behaviors, you can start to reflect on the most effective use of your time. You'll have the autonomy to dig deep and ask, "what do I REALLY want?" Do you want to lose yourself in an afternoon of art? Go for a walk and breathe in the crisp air? Call a friend and laugh for hours over old stories? It's up to you to *choose* what feels right, take ownership of your experience, and RISE above.

TAKE TIME TO CONSIDER:

What in your life limits your capacity for bliss?

What are you not writing down because you don't want to admit it?

Would you feel comfortable "limiting" the limit's influence in your life?

What strides will you take to dissolve the limit's power over you?

What would you like to do with all this new time and space?

3

She is

NOURISHING HER SOUL

ONCE WE CONSCIOUSLY CHOOSE to stop feeding our egos, we have more than enough time and energy to feed and nourish our souls. Let's break this down.

Nourish: Google Definition: *"provide with the food or other substances necessary for growth, health, and good condition."*

Nourish: Haley's Definition: *"fill to the brim with the most glowing love and energy by turning inward, observing, resonating, breathing deeply, letting go, opening-up, and letting a childlike joy overcome you through laughter and self-expression."*

Soul: Google Definition: *"the spiritual or immaterial part of a human being or animal, regarded as immortal."*

Soul: Haley's Definition: *"The foundational energy of our very existence that connects us to all things, including: our spirituality, sense of oneness, connection to our religion, and the most sensational, joyful feeling we can reach for within."*

* P.S. – The homophone for 'soul' within its definition is *sōl - Spanish for "sun", and poetically indicative of the sun-like, radiant light within each of us that extends from our souls and soul connections.* Coincidence? I think not.

You know best what it takes to nourish your soul. You most likely do not need someone telling you how to shape your schedule, or eat, or work, to be the most fulfilled. Such details may differ from person to person. However, some general practices have been tried and tested over time. The following suggestions have worked for me and countless others. Play around to see what works for you!

WAKE UP EARLY.

I know, you want to skip this elaboration because, you think, "No way will I wake up early. That won't work for me." Let me just say: I was a night owl for the longest time, but I began to realize that after a long day, my energy was split between what I was doing and my thoughts. It was difficult to be present. Furthermore, I would have to sleep in late to fit in those healthy 8 hours, and found myself groggy through the afternoon.

Just try this one time: Set your alarm for 6 a.m., lure yourself out of bed with the vanilla latte / green tea / peppermint hot chocolate you strategically planned the night before, and enjoy it by an open window as the sun rises and its rays begin to stream into your room. Take time to check in with your body and plan for the day. Take time to read a few chapters of the book you've been neglecting.

Take time to knock a few items off your to-do list.

Morning is my favorite time of day because everything is quiet and still. There is a peace that fills the corners of a room that evades us in later hours. This peace allows our best selves to act in productive ways...especially because we are so well-rested when we awaken! *All* of our attention can be fixed on whatever task is at hand - even if it's just an extra hour you set aside to be creative. No one will be texting or calling, nothing will distract you. The morning can belong to you.

So often I hear "there are only so many hours in a day". Making use of the morning allows you to maximize your time. You'll be so tired when 9:00 PM rolls around that you won't have the energy to mindlessly scroll through your Facebook feed or lose track of intention in whatever else you do (your Pinterest boards won't mind if you skip them for the night, I promise). I was often dumbfounded by how many hours had passed reading trivial articles and stalking celebrities on Instagram. Suddenly it was 1:00 AM and I had nothing to show for my time except a deeper understanding of Jessie James Deckers' style. In short, we are generally most productive in the morning - and can direct our energy toward what we NEED to do - because our minds are clear (for some of us, after a little coffee, but nonetheless!).

SET ASIDE AN HOUR IN THE DAY TO DO SOMETHING YOU ENJOY.

Take the time to get creative, get messy, get down in the paint, run a few miles, or destroy your kitchen with chocolate-chip cookie ingredients. Do whatever feels fun and good for you on a daily basis, and embrace experimenting with different activities on different days. No matter how demanding your day is, take an hour for yourself. Let your thoughts run on their own, turn on your favorite songs and escape from reality. You will return to your daily duties feeling rejuvenated. Remember... life should be fun!

PRIORITIZE HUMAN CONNECTION.

Commit to community building. Engage with those around you. Ask people about themselves. Listen intently. Share stories. Offer your assistance when needed. Indulge in laughter and mutual enjoyment. Speak of your dreams so friends and associates can hold them in their vision, too. Sharing your dreams with others multiplies the energy surrounding them, and draws their realization toward you.

> *"Ever talked with someone until you are no longer you? And they, not them?*
>
> *Until you forget your form. Begin to float. Become ideas. Dancing."*
>
> -DONTE COLLINS

LAUGH!

I must mention laughter because it is so important. Not only is it one of the best feelings ever (until something is just way too funny and you're on the floor and frankly, it hurts and you want to stop), but it releases serotonin and improves health. What more can you ask for? Romantic comedies, pictures of animals with dramatic personalities, videos of news bloopers (you must look this up), and the thousands of new memes in your Instagram and Twitter accounts can get your laughter going and your spike your mood. Your soul will overflow. Have you ever noticed how laughter is contagious? It is also a way to spread joy to others. If you are fully immersed in amusement and humor, the energy surrounding you affects those nearby. Create a fun-filled, giddy moment of collective laughter and joy!

GET MOVING.

Personally, I do not enjoy exercise, so I find ways to improvise. My best friends and I have dance parties, which are a surprisingly fun way to boost your cardio and enhance your confidence in your moves for whenever you have to dance, like, um, yeah — in front of people. Yoga is another great way to escape the hustle and bustle of daily life and find your center while doing wonders for your body. Take your dog for a walk, or your neighbor's dog if you don't have one (they'd appreciate that). Try out community kickboxing or an aerial yoga class. Aim to get your heart pumping and blood flowing just once a day. It will naturally energize you and push you to an endorphin high, which is even more fun when you know how much good you just did for your body.

GET CREATIVE.

When we immerse ourselves in the creative for a while, a warm and buzzy space envelops us, energizing us. Make it your prerogative to attain this space once every few days. Look through magazines, cut out words and pictures that speak to you, start a scrapbook. Get an adult coloring book (or a kids' one is good too, if you're feeling reminiscent) and lose yourself in crayons and colored pencils. Write, and be open to whatever comes out. Do it for you and for no one else. Expect to keep it for your eyes only so your true creative genius can be unleashed without the pressure for it to impress. When we create, we claim our space. It's a way of saying, "I am here, and I have something to express." It is an act of love. Your soul will thank you.

> *"Art is the only way to run away without leaving home."*
>
> -TWYLA THARP

DO SMALL ACTS OF KINDNESS FOR OTHERS.

This piece of advice comes from my mom, and she added something very important: don't tell anyone! These are SECRET small acts of kindness! If you expect praise for these small acts, that gets you right back to your ego. Here are a few examples to get you thinking...

Pick up the empty soda bottle that has been sunbathing on the sidewalk for a week, and throw it in the trash. It will make someone else's walk more pleasant.

Put money in an expired meter. Saving that person from a ticket will make their day, and give you good parking karma!

When you go through a drive-through, ask to pay for the next order. The customer behind you will never know more than what the back of your car looks like, but you'll know you made their day and sparked a desire within them to "pass it on".

> *"You have to be the kind of person who can make the best out of a Tuesday.*
>
> *Those living for the weekend are wishing their life away."*
>
> -DREW MARVIN

We are so often walking in a haze, preoccupied with our own agendas and our own problems. Taking a moment to care for others can halt whatever narrative has been repeating. It's intentional and heartfelt, and it truly does change how you feel about yourself. If you take these steps to nourish your soul, every day will exceed your expectations and continue to fill you to the brim.

I'll end here with the lyrics of one of my favorite songs, *Glow* (ft. Jeremy Zucker) by Justice Skolnick:

"Girl, you got that light."
YES, YOU DO!

How can you take more time to nourish your soul? What sounds fun? You deserve it!

4

She is

MAKING HEALTHY CHOICES

FEATURING KELLY HART

FOR THIS TOPIC, I'd like to introduce my dear friend Kelly Hart. Kelly is a certified reflexologist and wellness guru dedicated to helping people realize their optimal physical, mental and emotional wellbeing. She is a wealth of knowledge regarding nutrition and gluten-free living, and was another influence in my life to try yoga. Kelly is also my partner in bringing the organization She Is Without Limits to life.

HHS: I'd like to start by talking about my experience going "gluten-free" for a while. It was prompted by months of discomfort - brain fog and constant exhaustion were the most robust. No number of espresso shots could get me out of that funk, so I decided to eliminate gluten for some time. It worked, and prompted more research into the impacts of gluten. I can't help but think: if some individuals have such a strong negative response to gluten, isn't that a testament to how unhealthy it is? When I consumed it again, a subtle nausea stuck around and my energy plummeted. I've heard of individuals having similar experiences after returning to sugary drinks or even meat. I interpret these responses as an indicator of just how *bad* some of these ingredients are for us... and some of us will never come to know the full extent of the damage we are doing to ourselves, just by lacking an education about what we are putting into our bodies. What dietary restrictions do you recommend girls and women try for a few days, just to experiment?

KH: I don't blindly recommend dietary restrictions. Moderation is still a good general rule. That being said, food allergies and sensitivities in the United States have increased dramatically in the last twenty years. Now our food production is more scrutinized. As a society, we're becoming more conscious of where our food comes from and are demanding higher standards for ingredients and labels. It's really great!

There are legitimate conditions for which a gluten-free diet is *necessary*, like celiac, and there are conditions for which a gluten-free diet is *extremely* helpful, like autism and various autoimmune disorders. Some people choose to eat gluten-free simply because they feel better.

Your body is designed to communicate when something is wrong. If you notice a reaction after eating a particular food, (i.e. extreme bloating, discomfort or fatigue), try eliminating it for a while (2-3 weeks) and pay attention to how your body responds when you invite it back in. Elimination diets are a first-step proactive measure we can take to identify food sensitivities. Your body will send messages when something doesn't agree with it.

I encourage people to read labels and be mindful of what they put into their bodies. Remember that the purpose of food is nourishment. What we eat impacts our mood, sleep, and energy levels. When we don't feel well, it can usually be traced to the gut. Imbalances impact our immune system, allergies, asthma, even the condition of our hair and skin. Toxic systems lead to all sorts of problems. Sugar, specifically, is one of the most damaging things in our diets.

HHS: Oooh, sugar. I believe there is such thing as a "sugar hangover." I am an avid Whole Foods lover, but their gelato gets me every time. One night, I decided to treat myself to gelato after a particularly health-conscious and stressful week. One thing led to another, and before I knew it, I had absentmindedly consumed the entire carton. I didn't think much of it except "NOTE TO SELF: I need to pick up more tomorrow" - until the next morning I woke up with a real and true *sugar hangover.* My head ached, my stomach hurt, and the infamous "brain fog" that has haunted my life returned. I was utterly unproductive for the entire day, resolved to stay in bed, not even feeling well enough to haul my aching body to the yoga studio. Who knew a carton of gelato could do such damage? .... Kelly probably did.

KH: Ha-ha, I did, but only because of my own personal experience. Before health and wellness was my career, I had a sugar addiction and didn't even realize it. The state of my health and physical body changed drastically over the course of a year. I had always been physically active, but when I started writing at a local coffee shop every day (and buying caramel lattes!!), my sugar intake increased dramatically. My body wasn't happy. I noticed changes in my sleep and energy level, and my weight was increasing. It felt like someone had turned off the switch on my digestion. My system was struggling to absorb nutrients and eliminate toxins. I went to a GI specialist, but my blood work didn't indicate any problems. I was told I was fine and sent on my way. But I still felt off. I knew my body wasn't functioning optimally. Thankfully, I found a nutritionist who was able to help. That was a big lesson for me to follow my gut (ha!) and find the answers I needed to self-correct.

HHS: I used to be under the illusion that if you ate what you wanted when you wanted, your relationship with food would be so positive that it couldn't have a detrimental effect on you. Ha-ha. That is such a myth. It is okay to respond to our body's natural cravings, but I've explored healthier ways to do so. Example: my guilty pleasure is brownies. A healthier choice is choosing flax brownie chocolate muffins from Whole Foods instead. Same taste, same texture - except I'm putting nutrients in my body rather than processed flour. Another downfall with cravings is the use of artificial sweetener - when we taste something sweet but do not receive the sugar, our craving for sugar continues and intensifies. I have challenged myself to make my tongue "forget" what it once loved so much (Krispy Kreme donuts come to mind - talk about a heartache). I asked my friend Sarah how she overcomes the urges to devour the cupcakes, baguettes, and cookies we run into on a daily basis. Simply put: she knows how eating them will make her feel. It isn't worth it. This channels our willpower, girls - immediate gratification with detrimental long term results does *not* set the precedent for a loving relationship with ourselves.

KH: Indeed. Cravings are legit! And one of the biggest

challenges we can face, when it comes to healthy choices. Studies show sugar is more addictive than cocaine. Keep in mind that anything we put into our bodies can trigger a neurochemical response (sugar, for instance, stimulates dopamine, which in turn, makes us crave more).

When I was growing up, I was only allowed to eat "sugary" cereals on the weekends. I think it was a good rule. "Sugary" cereals ended up being a treat because discipline was a part of our daily lives. Plus, we didn't develop cravings.

Luckily, there are a few ways to combat sugar cravings if you're currently challenged by that cycle. Eating fruit or sweet potatoes, for instance, quenches your craving with natural sweetness. Eating sour foods, like kimchi and other pickled vegetables, helps bring balance to your palette. Keeping your blood sugar level by eating protein and fats helps you avoid a "crash". Sometimes it's as simple as slowing down and paying attention to what you're eating (mindful eating).

HHS: Your ability to recognize cravings reflects your ability to listen to yourself. Remember that you have a choice. Indulge in the craving, or satisfy yourself through other means. Love yourself enough to think critically about what you're putting into your body. Take ownership of your experience, and choose to feel *better*. The power is in your hands to make changes for yourself.

You can start by "playing" with your choices. How fun is that? Consider making the following changes to your routine:

"This week, I'm going to replace my Diet Coke at lunch with a sparkling water."

"This week, I'm going to try a gluten free cookie dough

for girl's night instead of the standard brand we usually get - I bet the girls won't notice!" (Actually - they might, and may even like it better.)

"This week, I'm going to avoid red meat and opt for chicken or seafood instead."

KH: Self-love is at the core of healthy decisions. It's so important to know yourself and your body, and to identify what foods (and habits, for that matter) make you strong and fierce. Emotional eating affects millions of people. We have the strength to overcome the mental battle and find our true power. I have personal experience with both emotional eating and honoring / loving my body. Whether you spend a lot of time thinking about food (overeating or avoiding it), or experience shame or guilt in conjunction with eating, your relationship with food generally reflects the state of your mental health. There are plenty of resources available if you think you need help. For additional information regarding eating disorders, please check out the following websites:

National Eating Disorders Association (NEDA):
www.nationaleatingdisorders.org

National Association of Anorexia Nervosa and Associated Disorders (ANAD):
www.anad.org

Binge Eating Disorder Association (BEDA):
www.bedaonline.com

The biggest take-away here is to be mindful and listen to your body. Connect with it. Honor it. But try not to obsess it over it. You'll miss out on so much fun if you restrict yourself too much!

HHS: One thing I want to touch on is the overwhelming

amount of information regarding health online.

KH: There is so much information at our fingertips, and new studies are released almost daily. These studies seem conflicting at times. Medical websites can be helpful as a reference, but I'm not a huge fan of self-diagnosis. So many factors play into what someone's symptoms are trying to express. The same set of symptoms in one person can mean something wildly different in another person.

HHS: To respond to your comment on self-diagnosis - ha-ha! I had myself *convinced* that I had celiac disease when I decided to eliminate gluten from my diet. Although it's not the best thing to put in my body - I've confirmed that for myself - I've also confirmed that I'm definitely not celiac. WebMD will get ya. People can convince themselves they have any allergy or disease by finding relevant information on the Internet.

KH: Ha! I've done the same! Professionals in any field are there to be utilized. There's a lot to be said for their knowledge and experience. We're making great strides in healthcare today. I've had an opportunity to study various alternative therapies and have broken down my own limiting beliefs about what we can accomplish naturally (everything from eliminating anxiety to beating cancer). Other countries have embraced alternative therapies for decades, but the United States is coming along. We're seeing more doctors who are open to, and even recommending, yoga and meditation for anxiety (now that studies prove their effectiveness). It's so wonderful to be merging Eastern and Western philosophies. There's a time and place for both.

That being said, prescription drugs and invasive surgeries

should be the *last* resort. We're accustomed to immediate gratification in the US, but our bodies will normalize if we do the right things over time. I've had young clients come to me with severe anxiety and panic attacks. The prescription drugs they were put on did more damage. In the end, they completely eliminated their anxiety through natural therapies like counseling or brainspotting, reflexology, journaling, aromatherapy, or exercise. It took anywhere from 2-6 months of dedicated effort, but they were able to learn how to manage their symptoms, and eventually completely eliminate their anxiety.

At the end of the day, assuming you're healthy, the keys to maintaining physical well-being haven't changed over time: drink plenty of water, eat nourishing foods, exercise, and pay attention to what your body is trying to tell you. Honor and value your body. It is intelligent and beautiful!

HHS: And all body SHAPES are beautiful! We are not all supposed to look the same and achieve the "perfect body." Looking healthy does not entail being thin and toned. I can tell someone is healthy regardless of their jean size because of a light that shines from within. I'm a sucker for "under-eyes", because typically I look so exhausted with swollen bags. I've noticed that the healthiest, most hydrated, and most nourished individuals radiate with confidence and beauty. My favorite compliment is, "You look like you've been awake for a while." In my mom's words, we are "bright-eyed and bushy tailed" when properly fueled by all the HEALTH we are putting in our bodies!

5

She is

LEARNING TO LET GO

ONE OF THE GREATEST CHALLENGES we face is knowing when to keep trying and when to relinquish control and let go. The practice of letting go always seemed passive to me, whereas being in control was active. I always wanted my hands clenched on the steering wheel of life. I refused to close my eyes and leave anything up to chance. What I realized, as most "control freaks" come to realize, is that being in control is merely an illusion, and makes accepting the unexpected much harder.

When we refuse to relinquish control, we're usually convinced we know what is best for ourselves. Think back on something you wished for that didn't come to fruition. In retrospect, you may realize something better took its place. Think back to when you achieved something you thought you wanted, but it didn't turn out as planned, or ended up leading you astray. Letting go tells the universe what my mom always reminds me: "This, or something better."

The desire to control puts you in resistance to life rather than moving with the flow. I believed I could mold my life by micro-managing it; but instead, circumstances molded me. The need to be in control is not just a sign of being ego-driven, but a sign of deep-seated insecurity. When you are secure in yourself, you are open to the flow of life. You are open to whatever comes. This type of "letting go" is an attitude toward life.

In learning this (a trial and error process, let me assure you) I wrote this quote on my wall:

> *"I let it go. It's like swimming against the current. It exhausts you. After a while, whoever you are, you just have to let go, and the river brings you home."*
>
> - JOANNE HARRIS

Learning to let go means releasing your deepest fears and embracing life. It's coming home to yourself, building a foundation within your own frame. There is no need to look further than yourself to feel stable. You can then let go of the way you want something to be and accept how it is, or be open to how it will turn out. Contrary to my prior belief, letting go is a very action-oriented approach to life. When we let go of desperate desires, we are ready for what life offers. It's our way of saying, "Bring it on, I can handle anything."

Of course, it seems that once this is finally implemented, the flow of life brings more of what we desire than what we don't. If we change our attitude to truly be okay with whatever happens next, whatever happens next is in sync with that energy. You no longer have the uphill struggle as you exasperate yourself trying to force things to happen. You have peace.

> *"I am tired of trying to hold things together that cannot be held.*
>
> *Trying to control what cannot be controlled.*
>
> *I am tired of denying myself what I want for fear of breaking things I cannot fix.*
>
> *They will break no matter what we do."*
>
> -ERIN MORGANSTERN, *THE NIGHT CIRCUS*

Sometimes, we think for the hundredth time, "If I just do more / wait longer / hold tighter, it will finally come." We work, push, and fight until we are exhausted, convinced we're in control. It is especially hard to let go when you've worked hard to achieve something. For example: getting into your dream college. How do you simply "let go" when you believe there is more you can do?

I know this from personal experience. Stanford was my dream school, and I was desperate to transfer there. Although they only have a 1% acceptance rate for transfers, I was convinced if I just worked hard enough and believed with enough fervor, I could beat the 99%. My desperation to attend Stanford began to entirely deplete me of my own individuality. An "all or nothing" mentality developed... my entire happiness hinged on being accepted. When I opened the rejection letter, waves of heartbreak crashed over me. I was crushed. It felt like everything I'd worked so hard for was destroyed, at the hands of strangers. The admissions committee never met me, yet I put my sense of worth and ultimate happiness in their hands. It took several days for the sting of disappointment to subdue, and then the exhaustion set in. I'd spent two years working narrow-mindedly for something that had a whopping 1% chance of coming to fruition. I had given it unprecedented power over me. And it suddenly dawned on me (while I was in the shower, where we all know some of the greatest epiphanies occur): although I had visited Stanford's campus twice and memorized every fact about it, did I *know* it was the right place for me? Or did I just *want* it to be the right place for me? I had romanticized it to a point of obscurity. The danger in idealizing is just that: your perception may be so far off from reality that the heartbreak is in recognizing the truth. The morning after I truly cried my last tear and let go of (my perception of) Stanford, I received my acceptance letter to Brown - which has turned out to be, in every sense of the phrase, "meant to be."

My hard work wasn't in vain, but I ruined three days of my life believing that it was. I ruined the three months beforehand believing my life would be over if I didn't get accepted. If you live and breathe thinking only one course in life will bring you bliss, you will ignore open doors and run to the closed ones, tugging on the handles, desperately trying all of your keys.

It is no secret that we are creative beings (men, too!) - but women possess the truly awe-some ability to give birth and bring life. This means whatever we create - even if it is just the mere *potential* of something - holds the same energy as something that has already manifested. Think of it this way: you're in a relationship with someone, and all signs point to marriage. In your head it plays out in a certain way: the dream proposal under the Tuscan sun (yes, that's a movie reference) to the princess dress at the fairytale wedding. Mentally, you are sprinting, guns blazing, towards this potential. And, should the relationship end, you aren't just breaking up with the person, but also with this potential future reality that never happened. That doesn't mean it wasn't real to you. And now, you must grieve what you wanted in much the same way that you grieve what you actually had.

So, give up that urge for control. Use your truly AWE-some female creative energy to create a future you want — but take away the specifics. I wanted the best undergraduate experience possible, surrounded by students who love to learn as much as I do, taking the most fascinating classes with the most esteemed professors. The specific of Brown University never once appeared in my potential future reality. And yet, it is fulfilling the non-specifics in this *actual* reality. Rather than naming the exact school, job, person, award, outcome, etc. that you want, imagine how it will make you *feel*. If you attract the *feeling*, you know whatever comes won't let you down. You know you can create that feeling and keep it, regardless of external circumstances.

FORGIVENESS

The other type of letting go is in our relationships with others. Inevitably, as humans, we hurt one another. We may be victim to vicious words or heartless actions that leave us in the bondage of hatred and resentment. Think back to any time you've been the perpetrator. When we lash out, it typically says more about us and the pain we are coping with than it says about the other person. It should be understood that when others lash out at us, it is more about them, however personal it may seem. As Buddha said, "Someone who truly loves themselves could never hurt another." Once we understand that everyone is learning to love themselves on their own journey, we have the foundational understanding to try to forgive.

Huge point here: Forgiving someone doesn't necessarily mean they deserve your energy going forward. Honor yourself, and exercise caution. Sometimes, when we check ourselves, the answer isn't pretty. It may reveal that we're lonely, or still have feelings for that person. Hey, at least you looked. Decide whether you want to repair the relationship, or simply forgive and move on. The true power of forgiveness, after all, is releasing any negative energy that does not serve YOU.

A (NONEXHAUSTIVE) LIST OF WHAT TO LET GO

◆ Outdated mindsets that no longer serve you. Negativity is exhausting, and at the end of the day we have a choice. How do we want to interact with our daily life? How do we want to envision our goals?

◆ Assumptions rooted in insecurities. I often hear, "Change the way you look at things, and the things you look at change." Have the courage to clarify rather than assume. For example; a yoga teacher once shared that, after sending out a personal, heartfelt email to her mailing list, she saw that a friend of hers immediately unsubscribed. She marinated in this for a while, feeling hurt. She decided to simply ask her friend for constructive criticism regarding the email. Her friend replied enthusiastically, reassuring her that she had switched email addresses, and only unsubscribed because she was already subscribed on her primary email!

- People who make you feel less than you deserve to feel, or *make you feel that you are hard to love*. You should not have to prove your worth to anyone. You deserve to feel loved and validated always, by all people. If you experience hostility in your relationships with others, it is a sign of discord within them. Wish them well - let them go.

- Situations that are long over and people who are long gone. Once you truly let go, there will be space in your life for new and better things. Life is a series of seasons. Sometimes we outgrow people or places. We are ever-evolving, and deserve to let go and grasp accordingly.

- Resentment and hatred. Another favorite quote by my pal Buddha: "Holding onto anger is like drinking poison and expecting the other person to die." I know what it's like to brew in anger and let it infect all of my thoughts. The other person remains unaffected, but my opportunity for joy and peace in the given moment is destroyed. Do yourself a favor and let go.

- Something that is just not working. I understand this is vague, but sometimes things are harder than they should be. Maybe it's apparent from the start. When you *really* want something — whether it's a job, relationship, activity, or conversation — but it's a struggle. Respect yourself enough to reserve your energy and LET GO. The right things come easily and go smoothly when you live in the flow.

As you begin to trust yourself more, you'll be able to make these decisions with more confidence.

CHANGING THE CHANNEL

These examples may have you thinking, "Okay, I need to let go of some things. But how?" It's easy to mull over lost loves, less-than-ideal situations, memories we want to replay and memories we'd prefer to delete. "Changing the channel" means releasing your thoughts and redirecting them to what you'd like to think about instead. How cool is that? We get to *choose* what we focus on.

So, every time a shadow of something I wanted to let go of flits across my mind, I simply replace it with something else, or concentrate on the present moment instead. There is no "OH NO, I THOUGHT OF IT. I AM STILL THINKING OF IT. I MUST NOT KNOW HOW TO LET GO!" C'mon girl, you got this. Change the channel!

Think about situations you held onto / tried to control for too long. What did it take for you to finally let go?

How did it feel when you finally let go?

What in your life would you like to let go of? (This can include people, situations, emotions, ways of thinking.... truly, anything.)

What steps can you take to let go?

Are you willing to let go? (Sometimes, despite our exhaustion and the knowledge that something is no longer serving us, we still are not quite willing to let go. It's okay. Remember, these are objective observations about yourself and there is no judgment toward what you are willing and not willing to let go of.)

If you are not quite willing to let go, why not?

MORE WAYS TO LET GO:

(BECAUSE SOMETIMES WE NEED TO PROCESS BEFORE WE CAN JUST REDIRECT OUR THOUGHTS)

These are tried and true ways to get the ball rolling.

- Write down everything you can about what you want to release. Go into obnoxious detail. Repeat yourself. Get angry. Then rip the paper into pieces, or throw it into the fire. The ceremonious act of destroying it helps you let go.

- Talk with someone you trust. Sometimes an outside perspective helps us understand what is blocking us from letting go.

- Be mindful of when it enters your thought process and what provoked it. Do not chastise yourself for thinking of it. Rather, kindly remind the thought that is has no place in your mind and should find the door.

- Vent about it to a friend. Vent about it in your journal. Vent about it to your cat. At a certain point, you will actually be sick of talking about it. And once even you are sick of it, you will be more than ready to finally let it go.

> *"Letting go gives us freedom, and freedom is the only condition for happiness.*
>
> *If, in our heart, we still cling to anything - anger, anxiety, or possessions - we cannot be free."*
>
> - THÍCH NHẤT HANH

6

She is

MOVING ON

FEATURING KELLY HART

For this chapter, I'd like to bring back my friend, Kelly Hart, to talk about everyone's least favorite topic — breakups! An inevitability of life is the fact that we will lose people. Breakups are natural, and somewhat of a "rite of passage". As much as they suck, they're important in the process of understanding who we are, and how we mold ourselves and change in certain relationships. I see now, in retrospect, how the breakups I've gone through have helped me grow into who I am today.

And who knows that better than my soul sis, Kelly Hart? Kelly has been there for me through it all, and vice versa. We've formulated the best tips and tricks for moving on from whatever breakup you're going through - whether it was a summer fling or ten-year engagement (like the movie).

KH: Breakups can be so painful, yet so important in tapping into our true power. The good news is: on the other side, you'll be a stronger, more bad-ass version of yourself! One of the most valuable things you can do is face the breakup head on, deal with it up-front. Learn to identify and sit with your emotions - don't be afraid of them! The more honest you are with yourself, the faster the process will be (plus your future relationships will benefit from not bringing baggage!).

Journaling is especially helpful. You may choose to provoke emotion via old songs, photographs, etc. Nurture yourself, and allow time to heal.

> "Be gentle with yourself. You are a child of the universe, no less than the trees and the stars...
>
> And whether it is clear to you, no doubt the universe is unfolding as it should."
>
> -MAX EHRMANN, *DESIDERATA: A POEM FOR A WAY OF LIFE*

Forgive yourself for your part in the dissolution. Self-loathing doesn't serve you. When I was going through my most difficult breakup, I adopted a mantra:

> "Forget the mistakes of the past and press on to the greater achievements of the future.
>
> Give so much time to the improvement of yourself that you have no time to criticize others.
>
> Live in the faith that the whole world is on your side
>
> so long as you are true to the best that is in you."
>
> - CHRISTIAN D. LARSON

That mantra gave me strength on days when it was difficult to get out of bed.

If you find yourself drifting toward negative self-thought,

reach out to a friend, or shift your focus to goals for the future. Mind control is important during a breakup. If you're feeling overwhelmed, get up and move. Go to the gym, go for a walk, or dance. Kickboxing is a great sport to take up during a breakup!

HHS: My best advice would be to shift the focus from grieving the other person to loving yourself and becoming your own cheerleader. In my last breakup, I missed his affection more than anything. I didn't know that I could rely on myself for the same affection he had given me. So, I changed my relationship with myself. Anything you go through presents an opportunity to understand and love yourself in a deeper way. We can do this even in the face of pain. Particularly, I'd commend myself on the small accomplishments - even if I had a horrible day dealing with my heartbreak, I'd look back and give myself kudos for making it through! Each day gets better, and if you aren't in opposition to the pain, you can lean into it and heal faster.

You may be thinking - What? Lean into the pain?

Resisting the pain or loneliness will only prolong the process.

Know that with every second that passes, you are working through it and getting stronger. That was one of the biggest things during my breakup: knowing that every moment of *literal* heartache was not for nothing.

I promise, as backwards as this sounds, that dealing with it upfront is the best thing you can do. Otherwise, it will fester beneath the surface and show up in subconscious ways. There is always the temptation to heal with another person - the "rebound" - but this, too, is a bad idea! Filling someone's void with another person won't help anything, because they won't fit that unique void. And - most importantly - you will always have a void, whether it's covered with a Band-Aid or left wide open. If you do not fill it with yourself, you will never be able to have a healthy relationship.

"Fill the void yourself" may sound like the most abstract advice ever, but what I mean by it is this: first we must allow the void. If you sit with that pain and trust, new opportunities will come. Insights and breakthroughs will happen. Inspiration will strike. Slowly but surely, that void will be filled, purely by your own intention to be whole and perfect on your own (which you ARE!).

KH: Yes! It's important to be comfortable being alone. Breakups are an ideal time to turn inward, a time for self-discovery! Often, when we are with someone for a while, we get comfortable and may be afraid to change. Breakups are a great time to try new things, take up a new hobby, or tweak your look. Devote time and attention to yourself. Get to know yourself on a deeper level.

> *"Ruin is a gift. Ruin is the road to transformation."*
>
> -ELIZABETH GILBERT, *EAT, PRAY, LOVE*

A release ceremony can also be helpful. This is a direct indication to the universe that you're releasing the old and making room for the new. First, write down the things you forgive yourself and the other person for. Next, write down several things you'd like to welcome into your world. Then, burn the piece of paper with the things you're ready to release, and bless the things you're ready to welcome in. Place your list in a space where you'll see it repeatedly. Release ceremonies are designed to help you release negative energy, detach from your ex and reclaim your power.

HHS: I also have to mention how NOT to deal with breakups on social media... and I feel equipped to advise in this area because I have made these mistakes! Bottom line: The breakup shouldn't be mentioned. You should avoid posting just to prove a point ("Look how happy / beautiful I am without you!"). It may be the best picture ever, and you may get twice as many likes as they ever got (HA!), and it may provide a short-term buzz, but ultimately, it is detrimental to your self-concept and integrity. Kelly always tells me the Ghandi quote: "happiness is when what you say, what you think, and what you do are in perfect harmony." (Good one, Kells!). If you put effort into a feigned facade to try to prove that you are happy, you will be unhappy. On the same side of the coin, you shouldn't be broadcasting your pain, either. Be honest with yourself and those close to you.

KELLY AND HALEY'S PERSPECTIVE ON POST-BREAKUP GROWTH OPPORTUNITIES!

- ◆ Align yourself. Recognize how you've changed and decide where you're going. This is a great time for goal-setting and focusing on yourself! Chances are, it's been all about him or her for the past however-long-your-relationship-was. Yay, it's YOU time!

- ◆ Sit with the void despite the discomfort. Just knowing that new opportunities are inevitable and WILL fill the gap will invite them in. Be open to what's new.

Embrace the evolving process.

- Shift your perspective: try to see the situation as a gift rather than the "worst thing that ever happened to you." Choose an empowered path rather than the victim role.

- Clean cut, cold turkey! Don't try to discuss the breakup with your ex (all over again, after the fact). Even if you feel there is so much to say, write it down for yourself only. You have a choice - you can marinate in it forever, or pull the Band-Aid off right away. And, no, contrary to some beliefs - you cannot be friends with your ex right off the bat. Find strength in solitude!

KELLY AND HALEY'S TRIED AND TRUE STRATEGIES FOR DISTRACTING YOURSELF POST-BREAKUP

- Yoga, kickboxing, any form of exercise! Just get moving - exercise keeps your chi flowing and keeps your energy from getting stale. Try not to wallow. We store memory in our muscles and at a cellular level. So, as we work out, we are processing and releasing events and emotions!

- Journaling. When it's just you and the notebook, you can be honest and raw. It's also healthy to channel your emotions in a private, safe space.

- Move into a creative space. Whether it's painting your white walls a vibrant magenta, or scrapbooking a gift for your longtime bestie, or planning a party - creative energy comes back tenfold and naturally makes us happier!

- Avoid alcohol or drug use — they cloud your thought processes and create emotional instability. You want to retain as much control as possible.

- Unplug! Put their number on "do not disturb", if needed, to avoid even *subconsciously* checking if they've texted or called. You can also rename them in your phone (so your heart doesn't drop when they *do* reach out), or be bold and delete their number. Their name, alone, can naturally provoke emotion. Don't go for that ride! (Kelly suggested I change my ex's name to an emoji of a man with a mustache. It helped!)

- Make a list of everything you ultimately want in a partner. Especially the qualities your ex lacked.

- Listen to empowering songs. Music helps us channel emotion and provides strength!

- Be intentional with how you fill the void, whether it be retail therapy (in moderation... set a budget, girl!), volunteering, or simply focusing on the other wonderful people in your life.

7

She is

DEMYSTIFYING PERFECTION

THIS TOPIC IS DEAR TO ME because of my own experience desperately trying to achieve perfection - an obsession that is shared by many. In the interest of being vulnerable, I'd like to share how I demystified perfection in my own life.

When I entered CU Boulder in my freshman year of college, I was determined to make the most of the year. This entailed taking advantage of every opportunity that slightly interested me and spending hours studying meticulously, even for quizzes.

My "Type A" personality was fueled by the inferiority complex I developed in high school. My mediocre high school performance led me to be terrified of less-than-impressive results. I suddenly needed to be the best at everything. Success began to matter more than my well-being. I was often asked, "How do you do it?" I didn't have an honest answer. I was doing it, somehow, but I was anything but happy.

By the time second semester rolled around, I was plagued by constant anxiety. I couldn't relax. I had to be on my game, pushing myself further. A test could send me into a paralyzing panic attack. In fact, I desperately tried to reschedule my Macroeconomics final exam at the last minute because I couldn't see straight. Anxiety leaked into every aspect of my life. I couldn't sleep. I couldn't go to lunch with a friend, because my heart pounding in my ears would overwhelm any conversation. I couldn't sit at dinner with my boyfriend without running to the bathroom to call my mom - "I just don't know why I *feel* this way", I'd sob into the phone. Laughter and any semblance of joy seemed rare and far between. My perception of my self-worth came down to an ultimatum: either I had to achieve perfection with a cherry on top, or I was worthless.

I finished my second semester with a perfect 4.0. I was awarded Student of the Year. I remember staring at the award, desperately trying to feel something. Instead of feeling a sense of accomplishment, I felt empty. Sitting with my parents at the celebratory, "goodbye freshman year" breakfast, I felt the waves of anxiety consume me. I drove home with my dad. He told me I could — and should — finally breathe. I had succeeded, but the inner turmoil remained.

And then it dawned on me. I had forgotten what is MOST important in life: Happiness and wellbeing. I was so scared of mediocrity and a life of insignificance that I drove myself to the point of insanity.

Success means absolutely nothing if you cannot truly feel happy.

There's no room for self-love or creativity in the space I

had created for myself. Sometimes we fail, or fall short, but it doesn't change our innate value and worth. It gives us more dimension; more wisdom for next time.

Happiness and well-being started, for me, with self-acceptance and forgiveness. Sometimes we make ourselves sick, whether it's physically or mentally (or both), and we need to give ourselves time to rest. We can reserve time in the day to put our heart and soul into work, but at the end of our lives, our GPAs and resumes do not amount to the joy we let into our lives and the ways we nourish our souls.

I may always feel a deep-seated need to push harder, be better, and improve. I may be disappointed at times when I inevitably fall short. But our many quirks, our favorite songs, and the connections we make along the way — those are the things that define who we are.

I wrote an email to a professor about something similar, and I will close with part of it:

> "I attribute my success in your class to *effort* alone. I am working on believing that it could be because of my intelligence. I am working on believing that *I am more than countless hours of studying*. I am working on challenging old beliefs about my possibilities and limitations to redefine myself. Maybe then I can take a deep breath, release some of this tremendous effort, and *trust what's inside of me*."

Perfection is simply an illusion. Imperfections make you, YOU. And, because of them, life is more colorful.

I choose that over perfection.

What do you choose?

8

She is

EMBRACING DIVERSITY

FEATURING SHUKRI ADDO

IT IS SO CRITICAL TO CONSIDER diversity in this content, because no two women live the same experience. The act of being authentic about our own lives entails being truthful about the ways that both privilege and disadvantage affect our stories. While it is the mission of She Is Without Limits to provide a platform for women of ALL backgrounds and circumstances, this chapter provides one perspective on this very important subject.

HHS: Meet Shukri Addo. She is one of my dear "long-distance" friends who shares a similar passion for female empowerment. She is the Founder and CEO of Chick Starterz (more on that in a later chapter!), who understands the need for women to power together and uplift one another. I'm delighted that she wanted to join me in this chapter.

SA: Thank you for providing the platform to share my experiences as a minority. As an African American woman who, further, looks different because of my hijab (headscarf), I have often found myself battling stereotypes, prejudice, and discrimination. My experience has often involved encounters where I've had to explain why I wear the scarf and whether I am forced to wear it.

HHS: Something I've noticed and talked about in a scholastic environment is the cultural polarization regarding the scarf. I've talked with, and read about, many women who feel they are at a crossroads, advocating for themselves in the feminist sphere, and wanting to honor their faith by wearing the scarf. The two shouldn't be mutually exclusive.

SA: Some of my early youth experiences involved direct and deliberate physical and verbal abuse by prejudiced people. I've had "go back to your country" shouted at me on multiple occasions. When I was in high school, I had a man aggressively tell me, "Take that thing off your head. We don't wear that here." I was standing on a packed bus, holding onto a pole right in front of him. Looking away was all I could do. However, the man stood up and proceeded to pull the scarf off my head. It was the most terrifying experience I've ever had. I wondered how a piece of cloth could create so much hostility and anger. I chose to honor my faith - which was, at times, a dangerous choice.

HHS: That story gives me chills (and not the good type). What it seems to come down to is this: the scarf can invoke fear in those who don't understand it, or associate it with something negative. Unfortunately, some people live their lives dictated by stereotypes which are seldom rooted in reality. Further, some Westerners have the mentality that women who wear the scarf are being oppressed, and that it *isn't* their choice. Perhaps we've seen images in the media that liken the veil to a prison. Some in our culture feel the need to "rescue" these women.

SA: It's unfortunate that some Westerners make this assumption. The scarf embodies the complete opposite for me. It is a representation of free will. It goes beyond image and physical appearance. It is an element of modesty and preservation, which is empowering.

HHS: It's helpful to hear what it represents to you. Please elaborate.

SA: The concept of modesty and physical preservation is not unique to the Islamic tradition. You see it in the Amish community, (nuns) in Christianity, and in Judaism. Many of these individuals cover themselves. However, the same prejudiced beliefs are not necessarily given to these traditions. Yes, some individuals within the Muslim community do practice extremism and force women to wear the scarf. I would be in denial if I didn't acknowledge this. But, likewise, all denominations and beliefs have extremists in their communities. Forcing individuals to wear the scarf goes against everything it actually stands for. Wearing the scarf is only one small element of spiritual practice. I started the practice in middle school and wore it on-and-off until recently. In my youth, I didn't understand why a piece of cloth was a barrier to basic human interaction, why it caused so much hatred towards me. Now I wear it more consistently because it signifies my spiritual destination and the self-awareness that I have reached.

HHS: Visual indications of a different faith or background sometimes influence people's perceptions. It's unfair for people to be judged based on stereotypes. It sounds like the scarf has a negative association for some people. These associations have nothing to do with you as an individual, and everything to do with perceptions and misconceptions about your faith.

SA: To me, the scarf was part of my individuality, my self-expression. It posed as a barrier because some people did not embrace diversity. Indeed, it had nothing to do with me. It had everything to with the other individual. Institutions are also facing these challenges. Inequality for women is systemic. Minority *women* are further vulnerable to these challenges. Minorities with visual indicators of their identities have an even greater challenge. Research has highlighted that when it comes to entrepreneurship, minority women have less access to capital and higher interest rates on loans. As a female minority entrepreneur, this was saddening.

HHS: Especially because your work aims to empower women in entrepreneurial pursuits. To empower ALL women. Discrimination is not tolerated in your efforts to empower the young female entrepreneurs.

SA: There's no room for discrimination. I recently held a conference on behalf of Chick Starterz, my non-profit which fosters entrepreneurship in young girls while also empowering women entrepreneurs. The conference was titled Breaking Down Barriers: Women in Entrepreneurship. We discussed the real-life experiences of women and their challenges as identified in the program. We brought together a panel of female entrepreneurs of all backgrounds, as well as male entrepreneurs. One panelist, a female African

American entrepreneur from Kenya, Sandra Brogdone, said the following, which stuck with me:

> *"I never considered myself a minority. Back home everyone looked like me and talked like me. I never heard the concept of minority until I came to the United States. Everyone kept saying minority but I didn't understand it."*

> \- SANDRA BROGDON, THE CEO OF ROLE MODEL MAGAZINE,
> *A MAGAZINE THAT HIGHLIGHTS THE INCREDIBLE ACHIEVEMENTS OF WOMEN.*

HHS: That is powerful. Diversity should be considered in terms of equal individuals with rich cultural backgrounds rather than in terms of privilege and disadvantage.

SA: Aside from the challenges, I've had some very positive experiences. Being diverse offers so much, and research supports this. For example, when companies have a representative number of women and minorities, they tend to be more prosperous. Conflict theory also holds that diverse teams and groups perform much better.

HHS: How has diversity allowed you to empower yourself?

SA: I have always felt that the challenges were relative. I looked to sources of empowerment from not only individuals who looked like me, but, also from any individuals who battled hardships and conquered them. I loved listening to motivational speeches, spoken word, and stories. I used all these tools to empower myself. I also had the realization that I was not alone in these challenges. Young women who identify with me may also have these challenges. So, I wanted to contribute to the pool of strong women who continue to make an impact.

HH: Prejudice disregards the individual. It is based on

stereotypes about a group, with no regard for the personality, hopes, dreams, and talents of the individual who shares the characteristics of the group. Strategies for breaking down prejudices include bonding together in community, being an ally to someone of a different background, and advocating for what you believe in. Racism, sexism, ableism, classism... every "ism" or prejudice loses its power when the "herd mentality" disintegrates. Love is stronger than hate, and the politics of LOVE can bond in a way that hate never can. We just need to mobilize the culture of advocacy.

9

She is

RESPECTFULLY SETTING BOUNDARIES

HAVE YOU EVER FELT depleted by or resentful of others? I have a hard time saying "no", and often give of myself so freely that I end up disrespecting myself. Sometimes I am angry with someone, seemingly unprovoked. Once I think critically about why, it is typically due to an absence of boundaries.

THE BALANCE

Growing up, I often felt the need to apologize to others. I wanted to be a good friend. I believed this meant constantly forgiving, even if the other person did something that didn't sit right with me. I always put it behind me, and pushed it down when it began to show its fangs. The thing about pushing down unresolved conflicts is that they will eventually come up again.

Beyond my susceptibility to forgive easily, I gave so much

of myself to others that I forgot about me. Perhaps I worried about being disliked or rejected by the people I was trying to please. So, I dropped what I was doing to come to anyone's aid. I spent nights consoling a friend who was fighting with her boyfriend when I should have been studying for a test. I stayed with a friend because she didn't want me to leave. Would turning my phone off or leaving my friend's house make me a bad friend? Denying myself what I needed or wanted made me a bad friend to *myself.*

It's tricky to discern when we are being compassionate and when we are over-gracious with others. It's the ultimate balancing act. Many women tend to self-sacrifice and are naturally empathetic. They feel compelled to give their time, energy, and support.

I am especially intuitive and receptive to energies that are not my own. Rather than setting clear boundaries, I respond to other people's requests with the same attention I give my own. I take on their moods. The result: resentment. I'm left feeling drained. I feel agitated when their name pops up on my phone. I wince when they say they have a question. I come up with excuses why I am busy before they even ask if I'm free. The friendship slowly ends anyway, despite my initial desire to please.

Defining our boundaries does not make us cold-hearted or distant, it shows self-respect. At our core, we know when something within us needs care or attention. It is up to us to recognize the signs and give our best to ourselves. The bottom line: at times we must say "no" to others so we don't end up saying "no" to ourselves.

Iyanla Vanzant is a spiritual mastermind and author of many empowering books, such as *Tapping the Power Within*. She has her own show called *Iyanla: Fix My Life* (girl fixed my life!). She spoke with Oprah on Oprah's Lifeclass on this topic and said something I will never forget:

> *"You want to come with your cup full. My cup runneth over. What comes out of the cup is for y'all, what's in the cup is mine, but I have to keep my cup full."*

She calls it being self-FULL rather than selfish. When we are full to the brim with the love and empowerment we have given ourselves, we have more than enough to share with others.

THE ART OF SAYING NO

Imagine if you asked a friend for something and they politely said, "I really wish I could, but I need to take some time for myself this afternoon."

I'm willing to bet that even if it wasn't the ideal response, you would respect the person's ability to say "no" (some women feel compelled to share a myriad of reasons WHY they're saying no, apologizing profusely, rather than just saying "No."). It's uncomfortable *hearing* no because we often wish we hadn't asked in the first place. We may feel like a burden for even asking, or rejected when they politely turn us down. These feelings are unnecessary. Another person saying "no" is an indication they are clear with their own boundaries and communicating *their* truth. Sometimes another person demonstrating self-care inspires us to do the same.

THE ENERGY TEST

This is about tapping into our emotions and cultivating self-awareness. We all know the feeling of heaviness. It's the "I don't want to" feeling of dragging your feet, like when you have a six-page paper to write but the sun is shining outside. Now imagine a lighter feeling, almost liberating, and absolutely satisfying. It's the cozy afternoon indoors with hot chocolate. It's fun. It's carefree.

You know these two feelings well. The Energy Test involves taking a moment to check in. When someone asks something of you, check the weight that you feel. Is it heavy? Are your eyes getting droopy? Are you imagining a Starbucks with four shots of espresso?.... Or, is it invigorating and exciting? The Energy Test can be used at any time. Be mindful of when you feel exhausted and when you feel invigorated. Our day-to-day experience can be dictated by the energies we uncover and allow in.

"QUID PRO QUO"

"Quid pro quo" is Latin for "something for something". At times, you may feel like a friendship has become an obligation. Because you have a history, or share mutual friends, it can be hard to break away.

It's natural to drift apart from certain friends. If the person can benefit from constructive feedback, by all means share it. In some cases, parting ways doesn't require a word. You both just know. The texts and calls dwindle, seeing each other on campus or out-and-about turns to a courteous exchange of words. This may seem sad, but it's part of keeping boundaries and growing up.

10

She is

EMBRACING HER VULNERABILITY

ON THE DAY I MET MY FRIEND KAITLIN, something remarkable occurred. We bared our souls to one another. We had just met - but every thought, every fear, all our secrets were disclosed. Imagine how empowering it is when two people come together and share every gruesome detail of their story. Kaitlin and I connected through our stories. We were vulnerable, showing respect for one another and ourselves, allowing for the most sacred "soul-sister" bond.

We often go through life with our two selves: our exterior selves, what we're comfortable showing, and the authentic self, which we only show when we are vulnerable. Can you imagine if you merged these two selves and didn't censor your speech or try to manage other people's perceptions? Can you imagine if you lived every day expressing yourself freely?

I see the exterior self as the rough outer shell. We are often judged by how this appears to others. We are selective about what we share with the world. We put effort into our superficial appearance. It's ok to have fun with the exterior self, if it's rooted in self-expression (rather than feeling pressured to look / act / be a certain way).

Have you ever felt exasperated or bored with a situation, or even your life, and decided to make an external change? Perhaps you indulge in "retail therapy", buying a different style of shoes or dying your hair. Maybe you feel like a new person for a moment. A few days pass, the new sparkle wears off, and you feel just the same as you did before the change. *You cannot alter your exterior self expecting it to improve your interior self.* The inner you still feels exasperated or bored once the external change wears off.

When we get vulnerable and real, we may recognize changes we need to make. When I'm with Kaitlin or my other "soul sisters", I'm authentic. I say what's on my mind and in my heart. I can truly understand the depths of my evolution, what I am going through, and where I am headed. I'm in a safe space, supported by friends.

Peeling away the layers can be scary. Are you afraid of what you'll see? Can you be vulnerable with yourself? Our subconscious is sly, and can emit self-deprecating thoughts. Recently, in a yoga class, an unbelievably critical thought came to mind. It sent me reeling. I could hardly focus on breathing because my eyes were stinging with tears. Within these cringe-worthy moments is the opportunity to get real. We can seek to understand where the critical thoughts come from, share them with friends, pull them from the root and watch them dissolve.

We get vulnerable and real so we can heal and be free.

So, if the exterior self is this rough outer shell, the authentic self is the gooey inside. It is loving and honest, full of grace. It deserves to to be explored, and allows us to connect with others in revolutionary ways. This connection is the best part of friendship and companionship because you know it is honest and real. It does not rely on altering your outer shell.

Being vulnerable allows us to connect with others in profound ways. We may find that those who came before us prevailed, and paved the way for the generation of women to follow. We may find that our soul sisters extend far beyond the friends in our immediate group. We may find that we are all connected, and support one another, in beauty and in tragedy.

Write about a time you were vulnerable around someone you trusted - it may be a friend or family member.

Write about a time that you allowed or inspired someone to be vulnerable around you.

Do you recognize a disparity between your rough "outer shell" and your inner "gooey vulnerability"?

What does "soul sister" mean to you? Do you have soul sisters in your life? If so, write down their names. (Contact these soul sisters now and thank them for sharing their insecurities with you and supporting you in the same way.)

11

She is

LEARNING TO LOVE HERSELF

THIS MAY BE THE MOST IMPORTANT TOPIC in this book - and one of the most empowering concepts you will implement into your life. We talk about self-love in many respects, in each of the preceding chapters. Merely taking the time to read this book is an act of self-love. It's a statement that you *want* and *deserve* to feel your best and live your happiest life. Heightening your self-awareness is self-love. Being introspective is self-love. Taking the time to answer the questions at the end of the chapters is self-love. So, kudos to you for that.

Self-love is a lifestyle. It's about releasing negative self-talk, critical thoughts, shame or guilt for things said and done. The desire to be better is normal. It pushes us to be our best. But we must also be comfortable in our own skin, and know that we are enough.

What if we just took the time to sit and be with ourselves? What if we committed to loving every facet of our personalities, souls, and bodies? What if we loved unconditionally, and always accepted ourselves? What if we chose to love ourselves as we are, today, no matter how insufficient we believe ourselves to be? There is no "I will love myself when..." because the only moment is now. I will love myself now. I will implement this self-love so deeply within my frame that it will never escape me. I will re-affirm this daily. I will correct any self-deprecating thoughts, but continue to love myself for having them.

I WILL LOVE MYSELF.

Spending time alone is critically important to learning how to love yourself. Relying on others for the love you deserve leaves a void that will never be filled until you focus on your relationship with yourself. It's intense, but taking time for this is critical. I'd like to share two deeply personal journal entries, as a reflection of the transformation that self-love inspires. These are timed about three months apart:

MID OCTOBER:

I miss simpler days when I didn't lean on my backbone as I do now. When I could fall into his arms. "Come here," he would say, and I would free fall. He would always catch me. And now I'm falling and falling and falling and I keep reminding myself that I am strong enough to catch my own weight, but when I release I collapse because it isn't him and I'm scared to rely on the tiny frame of this tiny body to give me what I'm used to receiving.

JANUARY 28TH:

Because it dawned on me: I loved myself. My tiny frame, this tiny body could lean on itself. My heart, despite any moments of weakness, could will itself to beat with fervor. My soul, however far it wandered at times, could call itself back home. I did not need the sweet words of an admirer or the physical presence of a loved one. I had all I needed within.

The biggest change I made in those three months was the way I talked to myself. I began to pay attention to my inner dialogue. Instead of chastising myself when subconscious criticisms appeared, I examined them to learn about my insecurities and opportunities for growth. I still find myself saying comforting words at times, soothing myself, rather than reaching out to others for support.

Try it for yourself! Begin replacing negative thoughts with ones full of love and acceptance. When you look in the mirror, whether you are fresh-faced or covered in sweat from the gym, say to yourself, "I'm a beautiful girl." Be your own biggest cheerleader. Dance inside creativity, knowing it is perfect because it is yours. Give yourself credit when you try, regardless of whether you succeed. Rather than justifying a mistake, accept what you learned. Forgive yourself and others, and let go of the pain. Listen. Know when to stop and when to push. Give yourself permission. When you need to sleep an extra hour, do it (without the guilt). If you want to treat yourself to a decadent coffee on a particularly stressful morning, take yourself on a date. Hold your own hand, hug your own frame. Love yourself, and step into your full power.

My dad always reminds me, "wherever you go, there

you are." You can guarantee that you will be with yourself for life. That's a long time. Dissonance within hinders your ability to live your happiest life, or give your best to the world. When you love yourself, you will thrive beyond your wildest dreams.

What do you love about yourself?

What are common affirmations you say to yourself?

Write down the first sentences / thoughts / phrases that come to mind when you think about your inner dialogue.

What words of approval and admiration have you always craved from others?

Take these words and tell them to yourself. Write them down and stick them where you'll see them. Hold your own hand, hug yourself. Everything you have ever relied on others for, you can do on your own. Space for thoughts:

12

She is

EMPOWERING OTHERS

ONE OF MY FAVORITE WORDS is "empowered". We hear and use the word all the time, in the context of giving someone the wings or guidance needed to take the next leap, or fulfill the best version of themselves.

I once heard a metaphor for women's leadership that perfectly depicts the concept of empowering others. Visualize us all climbing the symbolic "ladder of success". The woman at the top momentarily stops to reach below, and pull the next woman up. She loses nothing with this one pull. I imagine her saying, "I'm empowered. Be empowered too."

For those who tend to have a more competitive nature (group projects, anyone?), I know this can make you cringe. "But I climbed the ladder FIRST. Why should SHE get my help?" I'll just interject here to say - that, my friend, is your ego speaking.

We are all blessed with our own unique gifts, so we are not in competition. No one is a 'threat'. Competition squashes empowerment because you diminish what others accomplish in order to make yourself feel greater. Remember that other people's successes do not diminish *your* light. There is power in collaborating. And, believe it or not, contributing to others' successes actually empowers us.

I've worked hard to empower myself and those around me. I remind myself each day that I am a unique expression of love working in my own way to better the world. As are others. Feeling a larger responsibility (to humankind, or to the earth) enables me to listen more intently, understand more deeply, and use my intuition to lend wisdom when I think it will be suitable. And, I enjoy the process.

I remember attending an event called "International Coffee Hour" during my time at the University of Colorado - Boulder. I sat near a young woman who was truly extraordinary. She had such exquisite interests and passions. As I enjoyed my third piece of cake, I began to ask The Questions: Who are you? Where do you come from? Where do you hope to go next? Ah, how fun it is to ask another about their story.

I watched her eyes sparkle as she told me about her education. She was originally from Mexico, currently a senior majoring in Japanese. She enjoyed writing, and working with kids. It occurred to me as she was sharing, that she could write children's books in Japanese. I said it out loud, and I could see the wheels stop as she looked at me with a bit of disbelief. She told me she had always wanted to do that - and here I was, a stranger, telling her she could do just that.

Imagine if we all tried to be a little more mindful of how we engage with other women. Instead of comparing, get them talking about what empowers and excites them. Listen without judgment. We can empower one another to take ownership of our dreams and, in turn, make them tangible. "Tell me your story. How can I help you? How can I see power in you and encourage you to see, and be, in your full power?"

Empowered women empower women.
Empowered people empower other people.

Empowering others is void of ego. It is about active listening. An outside perspective is helpful when we feel stuck, or have perceived limitations. When we love others deeply, we want them to be their best and live the best lives possible. They aren't always aware of all possible paths. I'm open to the possibility that I don't know the potential of my best self, and someone else may notice my capacity for it (moms are the best at this!). The truth is, it's scary to stand in our full power! And yet, it's worth the try.

STEPS TO EMPOWERING OTHERS:

- Actively listen to what they say. This allows you to evaluate what they *perceive* to be their strengths and limitations.

- Repeat back to them what you are *hearing*. Be their mirror.

- Brainstorm opportunities. Provide options rather than suggesting a particular path.

◆ Give them the autonomy to figure out what course
of action they want to take. Remind them they can
break through any perceived limitations. They are
without limits!

**Write about a time someone said something that
empowered you. What did they say?**

**Write about a time you said something that empowered
someone else. How did it feel? What invoked you to say it?**

13

She is

A MOTHER AND A DAUGHTER

FEATURING HALEY AND TONYA KILPATRICK

HHS: I am so excited for this chapter because I'm introducing Haley Kilpatrick and her mother, Tonya Kilpatrick. Haley Kilpatrick is the CEO / Founder of the non-profit GirlTalk, which she began at 15 years old. Yes, you read that correctly - 15 years old. GirlTalk offers a program for high school girls to mentor middle school girls. I led a GirlTalk mentoring group as a senior in high school. It's an empowering program, and I've continued my relationships with many of the girls I mentored to this day. I've been thinking a lot lately about young people starting non-profits and recognizing that role models in our immediate lives have a huge impact. My mom is the one who encouraged me, from initial concept forward, to start Lit Without Limits. She gave me the courage to pursue my dream, and has not stopped being my number one fan along the way. Haley Kilpatrick has the same relationship with her mom. Haley and Tonya, I'll let you tell the story of how GirlTalk got started!

HK: The mother / daughter relationship can be critical to a young girl's confidence. My mom displayed confidence at a young age for me. That was key to me feeling I could approach her with what could be considered "far out ideas" as a teenager (my GirlTalk idea). My mom struggles with dyslexia, she's visually impaired, and she lost her brother and parents at a young age. I say this to explain that she didn't have a perfect life, but she was very confident and instilled in the three of us that if we believed, we could make things happen, and she would be our number one fan.

I remember as early as third grade telling her that a classmate, Robert, got his name written on the board for not having paper with him. We went to a school where many of my peers were impoverished. Instead of doing the traditional, "Okay let's go to Walmart and get him a notebook", she gave it back to me - "what are you going to do about it?" So, I came back to her two days later, with the idea to have a lemonade and popcorn stand. She turned everything into a learning opportunity, and I gained so much more from the experience than just going to the store with her.

So, when I got the idea to start GirlTalk, I knew she would encourage me and believe in what I could do. I say this knowing that a lot of girls don't have that relationship with their moms, but it doesn't have to be a mom — it can be *any* woman. The power of females, when they come together, is limitless. If only *every* girl could be so blessed to have a cheerleader like my mom, who could support me in taking action. I had to talk with the headmaster about my idea for starting GirlTalk. She didn't say she would do it for me or go with me. But she did sit me down to role-play and help me decide what to say. It made all the difference — because she's extroverted, I'm introverted — and I'm not sure my meeting with the headmaster to start GirlTalk would have ever happened. I just needed that little nudge.

HHS: Tonya, what has it been like watching your daughter succeed from such a young age?

TK: Watching Haley succeed at such a young age was not a surprise for me. I know this sounds cliché, but I felt like God was going to use her the minute they handed her to me in the hospital. Watching her genuinely care about others at such a young age was not a big surprise for me either, even though most tweens are only thinking about themselves. I knew God was preparing her for something BIG.

HHS: Do you have any ingrained philosophies regarding parenting?

TK: Philosophies regarding parenting are tough for me to talk about, because watching my daughter hurt inside and cry every day after school was not easy. As a parent, I was trying to understand what was going on with her and understand why all the other girls could not connect with her. But then I realized what was going on with Haley was what was going on with every middle school girl - it wasn't just her. That was tough on me as a parent to know and try to implement, but giving her the opportunity to figure it out on her own was KEY.

Haley began talking to a close family friend, a high school girl named Christie, twice a week after dance line practice. She grew to understand that Christie felt the same way in middle school. Haley slowly realize it wasn't just her. A beautiful thing began happening. Haley thought she should share this with all middle school girls, so they wouldn't feel hurt or left out. That's how she came up with the idea of Girl Talk.

HK: My relationship with Christie boiled down to the same notion of having an older influence - a mentor - in your life. I think what Christie was to me was what my mother wished she could have been for me. They told me all the same things, but I didn't hear it until Christie took me under her wing. It's a matter of shifting attention from our parents to our peers. Christie was very supportive, telling me I could get through high school. I'm very glad my mom never wavered in her commitment to being my mom to take on the role of being my friend, and was supportive of my relationship with Christie.

HHS: That is such a powerful story. I know it's a challenge for mothers and daughters to see eye-to-eye, especially on the important things. My mom, too, has always known when to let me figure things out on my own, and when to try to have a conversation about more difficult topics. Tonya, you knew Haley well enough to instill a confidence in her to do something about the misery she was experiencing during middle school. My mom did the same for me - she knew I would be a great mentor, so she sought out those opportunities for me. And when I realized how fulfilling that was, and how much I loved it, she supported me as I embarked on my own. Critical to this support, of course, is taking the time to connect with our mothers / daughters. Tonya, what recommendations do you have, and what worked for you and Haley?

TK: Something that worked for me was finding something that I was passionate about, and then introducing it to Haley. I thought introducing Haley to the Lions Learning Center in our hometown of Albany, Georgia would help her see how other kids struggle with everyday life. It also helped with my visual impairment. This would help her understand how difficult life could be. Haley volunteered there twice a week during middle school, and it gave us something to talk about - a common bond. Haley learned to teach a young lady how to read while volunteering there. This gave her a sense of purpose and helped her see another side to giving back to the community.

HK: There's an interesting turn when our moms, who we adored in elementary school, suddenly don't understand us when we're in middle school (or so it seems). During those years, it was so critical to find the glue that would hold us together and nurture the relationship. The service piece was huge in finding a way for us to connect - but also to get out of ourselves - because we tend to be very self-consumed in middle school. It was critical in understanding the broader scope of the world around us. It was also special to connect with my mom based on her disabilities, and to bring reading glasses to those impoverished. It made me appreciate my mom more - whereas, beforehand, I used to be upset with my parents for not buying me the latest Timberland boots or North Face backpack. They couldn't afford that, and I gained a greater appreciation for how much she did - for working, raising three children, being a super woman despite her visual impairment. I don't think I would've taken a step back to appreciate her without that service experience.

But, this doesn't need to be a huge commitment. It can be once a month, something different every time. It's also a great opportunity to engage other mothers and daughters to do something with us. I've seen how daughters have inspired their mothers and brought them into their service communities. You see moms get so excited, and it becomes this beautiful project. Something is ignited through service that is just so powerful, and from there, so much more beauty can happen.

HHS: I love that. My mom always looked for great volunteer opportunities for me, too. She fostered my heart of service. It's the reason I've become such a giver. She always reminded me of those less fortunate and spoke gratitude as a second language - for both our relationship and for all of our blessings in life. It's so important to be surrounded by people who ground us in gratitude and remind us of what is truly important, regardless of whether they're our mothers.

So, Haley, you're a new mom to a daughter. In what ways has your relationship with your mother spurred your philosophies in parenting your newborn daughter, Grace?

HK: My mom is such a source of strength, positivity, and love. I feel blessed to have witnessed those qualities my entire life, and to know that my mom sees the best in people. She loves all people - it's never about what she can get out of a relationship. My mom is always quick to serve - "how can I help you? How can I breathe life into your dreams?" It never stopped with us as children. It's the same with everyone she has met. I hope to draw on her strength, take on the lessons she's modeled, and share those with Grace. I will always have a beautiful, solid foundation. My brother and sister will too - it's been created through my mom. I'm excited for Grace to get to know my mom, if God wills. My mom has been known for reigniting the spark in people when they need it most. I'm so honored to call her my mom.

HHS: What a special love the two of you share. Thank you, Haley, for recognizing the importance of female mentors beyond our mothers. We have been so blessed to have the relationships we do, and it is critical to extend the same selfless love and encouragement to younger girls in our lives. Our mentors and role models play a significant role in shaping who we become; and my mom has worked tirelessly to instill the same confidence, self-love, and empowerment in me that you have instilled in one another.

TK: Thank you for this opportunity. I feel God has blessed me as a mother with Haley; and now Haley is helping other middle school girls tell their story, one girl at a time.

14

She is

CONSIDERING ENTREPRENEURIAL PURSUITS

FEATURING SHUKRI ADDO

HHS: For this chapter I'd like to reintroduce Shukri Addo. I met Shukri through a mutual friend, who suggested we get in touch because we were doing similar things. Without realizing it, at age 18, I became an entrepreneur when I began my non-profit Lit Without Limits. Shukri's non-profit, Chick Starterz, encourages middle school girls in entrepreneurial pursuits. When we sat down to talk about her work, a few realizations regarding women in entrepreneurship dawned on me. I invited her to participate in this chapter so we could hash out these ideas. Shukri, tell us about yourself!

SA: I grew up one of three females in a family of seven children. As a woman of immigrant background, business was never discussed as an option for a career path, especially as a girl. It was from a strategic point of view in having economic stability. As immigrants, we chose paths like medicine and engineering with linear structures and predictable outcomes.

Business was too risky and required investment and time, which most immigrants believed they did not have. I came to identify with nursing, as I have always wanted to give back and help others. Though business was never discussed, ironically, my mom raised us selling cookies and ethnic sweets on the side to earn extra cash. I used to help my mom and that's how I learned how to make cookies, which ultimately became my cookie business, Buskooty. My mom never referred to herself as a business woman. Similarly, when I picked up the cookie-making business in college, I never thought of myself as a business woman.

HHS: I experienced something very similar when I began Lit Without Limits. I wasn't a "business woman" or an "entrepreneur", I was just an 18-year-old starting a non-profit. I felt like you had to earn the title of "entrepreneur", and that non-profit organizations were not businesses. I still have discouraging conversations with individuals who don't see how a non-profit operates as a business, and therefore don't know how much effort, time and strategy go into its success. So, how did you move from making cookies to beginning Chick Starterz?

SA: It wasn't until recently that I began to identify with entrepreneurship and business. I couldn't get the idea out of my head - the cookies, the branding, etc...

HHS: I love that you mention that you couldn't get the idea out of your head, because it was the same with me for Lit Without Limits. I think we should encourage more young women to follow this inner voice. If you can't let it go, maybe that's because you're being called to do something. Anyway, continue.

SA: I began to read about business and branding and I was immediately propelled. However, in the pursuit of the cookie business, I began to get feedback as to how I did not have a business education, that I knew nothing about business, that I needed to have capital to start, etc. I was also told that I needed to get married and have kids because I was now educated and had a nursing career. The next step in my life, according to some of my family and friends, was marriage and not business. When people were telling me my business investment was a waste of time, the idea of Chick Starterz began. It began as a supportive platform to empower *myself*. I was watching videos of the stories and journeys of entrepreneurs to empower myself.

HHS: I say all the time that the work you put out into the world must resonate to have an impact. This resonance comes from a very personal place. I think we both felt that we had helped ourselves, and now were full to the brim with the capability and desire to use our acquired knowledge to help others.

SA: I felt the need to share some of the resources that were empowering me with the perceived women startups or aspiring startups. After creating Chick Starterz, so many women and girls encouraged me regarding my bold moves and passion. They shared their entrepreneurial ambitions and the barriers they were experiencing. I found myself being supportive and encouraging, both in private and public, on the Chick Starterz platform on Facebook.

HHS: It was an instant success, no surprise there. Listening to you merely talk about Chick Starterz is so enthusing. The first thing that struck me when I learned about it was the youth of the girls you are targeting. Can you speak more to your decision regarding that age group?

SA: As I began to engage with women entrepreneurs I began to get more exposure to the barriers of the diverse women in entrepreneurship. As I did more research, I learned that to bridge the economic and entrepreneurial gap between men and women, there was a need to start cultivating entrepreneurship in more young girls starting at the age of 11 years old. Girls of that age are capable and should be inspired to think in an entrepreneurial sense. Few already exist and we want to be part of building on that while using them as a model.

HHS: That seems to be a critical age. As we discussed during our first conversation, I realized that as a child, I wasn't encouraged in school to be an entrepreneur. It wasn't discussed as an option. As a result, I didn't consider it or talk about it. In fact, I didn't really consider my career at all. I remember wondering what job my *husband* would have. Rather than aspiring to *be* a CEO, lawyer, doctor, I would aspire to *marry* one. I'm glad we're moving away from a time when girls felt confined to the "straight and narrow" in career pursuits. Women are more encouraged than ever (from mentoring to grant money) to start their own businesses and create their own concept.

SA: Haley, you are right! Some girls are raised to be beautiful so they can be eligible bachelorettes for the potential "amazing husband" with the career and high socioeconomic status. They are hardly encouraged to pursue those paths themselves to gain their own economic independence. Some girls come from broken homes and end up seeking shelter in the hands of the wrong boyfriend who ends up supporting them financially but is also physically abusive. This is informed by my medical background. So many young girls are not provided the opportunity to explore their creative economic potential. With Chick Starterz, I want to facilitate that opportunity and create a platform for those girls and others who may come disenfranchised communities.

HHS: Perhaps the most unique consequence of Chick Starterz, as I see it, is the supportive aspect as well as the visibility of the women entrepreneurs you sponsor. Statistics don't lie: there are VERY few female CEOs in the spotlight. I often quote Madeline Albright: "You can't be what you can't see" - very true, but even seeing so *few* female CEOS of Fortune 500 companies is discouraging enough to totally alter a career path. We find comfort in setting aspirations elsewhere, and so in the public sphere these gendered jobs are perpetuated.

I want to conclude by saying that I truly believe we are all entrepreneurs in a sense because we all have something uniquely valuable to contribute to the world. Those who are entrepreneurs are essentially architects of this value. You don't have to start a business to be an entrepreneur - you can shape what you want to contribute to the world in an entirely different profession or discipline. Encouraging girls to think creatively and understand the massive potential their value has is incredibly empowering. It gives me chills just thinking about it.

15

She is

FINDING HER TRUE BEAUTY

WHEN I WAS EIGHT YEARS OLD, I was infatuated with Jessica Simpson. I kept a photo of her Christmas album cover by my mirror. I looked nothing like her. I was, well, eight years old, with mousey brown hair and brown eyes. She was fun and flirty, with tousled blonde hair and baby blues.

I remember my mom catching a glimpse of that photo by my mirror and frowning. "You know, Haley," she said, "That photo is edited. She doesn't *really* look like that."

That stuck with me for a long time. My mom's statement was so impactful that I still, to this day, do not compare myself to celebrities. Jessica Simpson lost her magic to me, and I retained my self-esteem. (No disrespect to Jessica Simpson, of course!)

External beauty is such an interesting concept, one that

has been over-emphasized to the point of objectifying women, and, at times, causing them to objectify themselves. Concomitantly, the desire to express ourselves and feel beautiful does not necessarily mean we are vying for the attention of men, or clinging to superficial ideals because we ultimately feel inadequate.

I love playing with my makeup and style. There is nothing like getting that box in the mail from Sephora, or trying on dresses at Nordstrom. It's empowering to me. Every morning, I spend time putting on makeup. I wear false eyelashes because they're dramatic and fun. I never tire of playing with eyeshadow. It is part of me - part of how I like to express myself - like how I love to write poetry or sing in the car.

We are all uniquely beautiful. The most beautiful women are those who are confident and know themselves - the most messy, real, vulnerable parts of themselves - and express that how they please. Beauty is in the eye of the beholder, and the only beholder that matters is *you*.

I find it beautiful when women cry, because it is powerful to express emotion. You are beautiful when you're covered in sweat with a purple face, emerging from the overheated hot yoga room. You are beautiful whether you wear layers of makeup everyday, or none at all. You are beautiful regardless of what you like to wear. You are beautiful if your style fits in, and you are beautiful if your style stands out.

Beauty, of course, is not simply external. It runs to the core. Growing up, my mom always complimented my curiosity, my compassion. Looks change and fade, who we are inside remains. And encouraging those innate traits is the best gift we can give one another.

Beauty is curiosity, and the constant desire to discover and learn. Beauty is kindness, generosity. It is asking what you can do for others. It is valuing your innate qualities - the way you write your "y"s, or your talent for sketching portraits, or the way you deep-belly laugh during those "had to be there" moments. The truest beauty of all glows from deep within, when you fall in love with who you are, and see everything you do as an extension of that beautiful, radiant light.

I found countless examples of admirable traits in characters I read about in books. This was part of the impetus in founding my non-profit organization, Lit Without Limits. I defined myself through bits and pieces of what I recognized in characters from literature. When we read, and begin to identify with the protagonist, we enter their minds and their hearts. This has nothing to do with their external appearance. In fact, we'll never know what they look like. What does translate, in a perfect language, are the relatable thoughts, characteristics, and quirky traits the character possesses. What also translates is a new dimension that has never been explored, enhancing our imagination, and probing deeper thought.

The beauty discussion would be superficial (ha!) if I didn't acknowledge that pressures from the media are real. It's important to recognize that media must SELL to survive. The images they share are overly-edited and photoshopped. The standard of beauty they promote is simply unattainable. Media will lead you to believe that there are quick fixes to achieving this "perfection". There are unlimited products you can buy, plastic surgery you can undergo... and everyone does Botox these days, right? The consumer market is inescapable, hungry for our money, striving to perpetuate our dissatisfaction further so we keep buying.

Around age 16, my mom took me to see the documentary *MissRepresentation* (by Jennifer Siebel Newsom and the Representation Project). It's a moving film that highlights the misrepresentation of women in the media, with commentary from many celebrities and scholars. This film (a "must see" in my opinion), in tandem with the Dove commercial about Photoshop, rocked the boat regarding my perception of magazine covers and billboards.

I chose this very topic when I was asked my junior year of high school to speak to a group of freshman girls. It was their lunch period, and they were required to attend this program weekly. I wanted to intrigue. I showed them the Dove commercial and several others, and opened the conversation. Everyone participated in the discussion because everyone could relate. Many women are affected by these photoshopped images, and the feelings of inadequacy they intend to provoke. One conversation can start to debunk the myths, and lessen the impact.

There's power when women come together as a group. Let's work as a force against these unnecessary pressures. Let's change outdated beliefs surrounding beauty "norms", because they're a hindrance to our ability to *feel beautiful.* Let's call out the media for the standards of beauty it idealizes, because we know *there is no standard of beauty.* Let's remind each other what we know to be true: that nothing external can define beauty, and the most beautiful parts of us glow when ignited by passion and love.

It's time to let it shine.

"i want to apologize to all the women i have called beautiful
before i've called them intelligent or brave
i am sorry i made it sound as though
something as simple as what you're born with
is all you have to be proud of
when you have broken mountains with your wit
from now on i will say things like
you are resilient, or you are extraordinary
not because i don't think you're beautiful
but because i need you to know
you are more than that"

RUPI KAUR

16

She is

PUSHING HER PHYSICAL LIMITS

FEATURING LAUREN SESSELMANN

I CANNOT TELL YOU HOW EXCITED I am to introduce Lauren Sesselmann: Olympic bronze medalist, World Cup champion, soccer player, entrepreneur, and one of my favorite humans! I pride myself on working out when I can fit it into my schedule (even though I honestly don't enjoy it!), but for this subject I thought it'd be more beneficial to hear from an athlete who has done it all.

HHS: Lauren, give us a peek into the daily routine of an Olympic medalist. What is your daily routine for working out and eating healthy?

LS: My daily routine varies depending on whether I'm in my season or not! When I'm in season, I usually get up around 6am and make breakfast. Breakfast is the most important meal for me because it gives me the energy I need to last through long and intense practices. I love making eggs, oatmeal with fruit, or protein pancakes topped with nut butter (those are my go-tos before games). I also drink a glass of water with my vitamins and have a little green tea for an energy boost. We always have a meeting before training to talk about what we want to focus on in that practice and we map out our goals for that day. We then go to the field and train for about 2 hours. After that, we have lunch, get treatment, have meetings, look at game film, etc. We'll get about a 2-hour rest, then it's back to practice we go. Our second session is either on field or in the gym, lifting to work on strength and speed. Our evenings are filled with dinner, treatment, meetings etc. and then we make sure we all get 8 hours of sleep. Then we get up the next day and do it all again!

When I'm not in season I try to enjoy myself a little more. I do a lot of soccer-specific training, but I also add in other fun workouts like swimming, kickboxing (my favorite) and spinning! In the off season, you put in just as much work, because that is the time to get even better. You should remember every day when you wake up to start your day with positivity and that you are going to leave everything out there in the gym or on the field. There is always someone out there working harder, so you must ask yourself how bad you want it. And eating healthy goes into that work. I say to enjoy everything in moderation, because I love me some desserts! :) Don't deprive yourself - just be smart!

HHS: I will take that advice on desserts! What are your tricks and tips for obtaining a fitness goal?

LS: I think for me, what I find that works is writing out my goals/ meals for the week. I'll sit down every Sunday and write out what my workouts are for the week or what classes I want to try out. I want to make sure I'm not overdoing it and that there is a balance between endurance work, sprint work, ball work, speed/strength work. I also find it works to map out my day: this time I'm doing emails, this time I'll be at the gym, meal time, time with friends etc. so it ensures I'm getting my work done but also enjoying life to the fullest. I always carry workout clothes and cleats in my car, which I find helps because it forces me to go to the gym when my energy is low. I also carry snacks with me everywhere. I never weigh myself because if I feel good that is all that matters. Scales always upset people and most of the time the number doesn't reflect how you look and feel. Case in point: in college, I weighed 160lbs and was a size 10. I didn't know how to take care of my body as well as I do now and I was lifting 30 lb. weights. I'm not saying that type of lifting is bad for you - that is what they had us do for soccer. After college, I learned different ways to train and became a faster and better player. I now weigh about 150-155lbs and am a size 6. I'm almost the same weight but my body looks completely different! You just need to find what works for you and what makes you happy, and you will notice changes. Just a note.... I was healthy at both weights and looked very athletic. No one would guess that was my weight. So, I say, don't let the scale deter you! Set your goals and smash them one-by-one. Things don't happen overnight - it's a process. But if you're setting yourself up for success, you will be successful.

HHS: What is the most important thing to remember while you're training?

LS: I think it's to make sure you do some type of dynamic warm-up beforehand and a good cool-down to reduce inflammation and injury, as well as recover quicker. Another thing to remember is to make sure you are doing different exercises correctly or you can hurt yourself. And, most important, is to always have FUN!!!

HHS: When we push ourselves past limits, it's hard to keep going when our body is SCREAMING to stop! How have you prepared yourself mentally for those hard moments?

LS: Oh, yes, I've had so many of those moments, especially towards the end of a game, or if you go into overtime. Soccer is a lot of running and a lot of stress on your body, both physically and mentally. What I find has helped me is mental training. I never knew much about it until I joined the Canadian National Team. We were lucky enough to have a Sports psychologist, which was extremely beneficial. I learned what works for me and what doesn't work for me. Everyone is different, so you need to find something that works for you. What I found worked for me was meditation and brain training. The night before a big game, I would sit down with the sports psych and let out anything I wanted to, negative and positive. He was there just to listen. Then we would talk about certain instances in the game or training that I was upset about or that I did well. I would then relax and play a brain game where I envisioned myself reaching all my goals in the game. He would say to me, "When you're tired, when you feel your body breaking down, what do you tell yourself? What do you do?" and we would envision ourselves fighting through it.

Between that and meditation, I find myself more relaxed when I step on the field. I find that inner warrior that never quits and leaves it all out there. A lot of us also have a "word", when you feel yourself failing in any way. You mess up a play, you are tired, you keep getting beaten... We look at each other and say the word, and it brings us back on task. Mine is "chocolate cake". I know it's an interesting word choice but it makes me laugh and brings me back to reality and makes me push even harder. Mentality is our biggest downfall in everything we do. We believe we can't do things, then we can't... We believe we can, and we succeed. You must dig deep in those instances and repeatedly tell yourself "You Got This".

HHS: That leads me to my next inquiry! I'd like for you to talk a bit about the inner dialogue as an athlete... because even though you play a team sport, being an athlete is very much about conquering the personal limits you believe you have.

LS: I touched on this in the previous question because this is SO important and crucial as an athlete, or in anything that we do in life. It's not easy. I will say that... there are days when I just want to give up, there are days when I have doubts. Everyone has those thoughts and those days, I don't care who you are... that's what makes us human. We are all scared of failing... it's in our DNA. Some people would rather not try, because they don't want to fail. I've learned some things the hard way and now have a better understanding of myself, so my inner dialogue has shifted.

Every morning, I've been trying to wake up with a different mentality. Yesterday is forgotten and tomorrow is not promised. What you do today is what matters. We have so little time - why not be positive, right? Every morning I wake up and say, "Today is going to be a fabulous day!" If something goes wrong, which it usually does (ha-ha), I now tell myself, "It's the not the end of the world... take a breath and figure it out", instead of getting upset. I get to training and I'm exhausted. Instead of doing less reps or cutting things out, I say, "Look, you have 1 hour to get better and then you can rest." Those little inner conversations help. It took me some time to get to this place, but I'm glad I'm there now because I'm enjoying life a little more now!

HHS: What advice would you give to someone who wants to start working out, but is out-of-shape and struggling with getting started?

LS: It's hard - trust me, I've been there! Even though I've always been active, I get in my slumps. I've seen my family and some friends struggle as well. We get to a place where we make excuse after excuse, or we are embarrassed, or just scared. It's not easy, but the reward is so great. It's amazing how much better I feel, how much more energy I have, and how much happier I am when I'm taking care of myself. You don't have to take a giant leap. As I mentioned before, set goals for yourself. Start going for a walk everyday. Grab a friend or significant other because talking along the way helps. I love going for walks and enjoying nature and listening to my favorite music or talking with someone. Walking burns a lot of calories. Start with 1-2 days per week, and then go to 3-4, etc., and then increase your minutes each time.

Take a good hard look at what you are eating. Start to make little changes here and there, like cutting your portions. I promise you will start to notice a difference and just feel better. Then, when you are ready, start adding some low impact strength exercises to your routine. If you need help, there are a lot of great workout programs online. You can use things in your house to exercise, or hire a trainer to help push you. I think the biggest thing is to believe in yourself, and make the time for it - 10 minutes, 30 minutes - whatever it may be, just do something little every day. In no time, you'll be doing more, and soon it will become a lifestyle! YOU CAN DO IT!!! I BELIEVE IN YOU!!!

HHS: Woohoo! How often do you push yourself to make sure you aren't just maintaining your shape, but getting more in shape?

LS: I think it's different as an athlete because there are different phases in the season when you push yourself. About 3-4 weeks before the season starts is when I ramp things up even more. I add a lot more speed and agility work to ensure I am fit enough to compete. Once we get to season we continue to build on the work we have already done and ramp it up even more. We work hard in the beginning to maintain throughout the season so your body doesn't break down. It's hard. You need to push yourself, and this is the time where that inner dialogue and help from your teammates comes into play. You're running 10 120's, and you want to lay down and give up. That's when your game-winning mentality comes into play. How bad do you want it? How hard are you willing to work for your teammates? Do you want that medal or not? Are you going to come in first place in the league?

I like to read one of my favorite quotes before games. I love the words and the meaning. It gives me so much motivation to work hard and reach my goals:

*"Our deepest fear is not that we are inadequate. Our deepest fear
is that we are powerful beyond measure. It is our light, not our
darkness that most frightens us. We ask ourselves,
who am I to be brilliant, gorgeous, talented, and fabulous? Who
are you not to be?
You are a child of God. Your playing small does not serve the*

world. There is nothing enlightened about shrinking so that other people will not feel insecure around you.
We are all meant to shine, as children do. We were born to make manifest the glory of God
that is within us. It is not just in some of us; it is in everyone and as we let our own light shine, we unconsciously give others permission to do the same.
As we are liberated from our own fear,
our presence automatically liberates others."

- MARIANNE WILLIAMSON

17

She is

EXPLORING THE STEM FIELDS

GROWING UP, I was a reader and writer (surprise!). I clung so tightly to these interests that I became rather narrow-minded. I cringed if I had to do anything science or "math-y". I was firm in my resolve: I was "right-brained". There was no way I could be good at the left-brain stuff. This "left-brain stuff" is typically referred to as STEM: Science, Technology, Engineering, and Math. I know many women who excel in STEM fields, and feel a natural affirmation with it. But I also know women who feel discouraged. Hopefully, this chapter will shed some light onto Women in STEM, and the extraordinary power we have to uplift one another in all pursuits.

I remember the first time I brought a bad grade home to my parents: it was a math test, a 78%. I was always a straight "A" student. I figured, "Okay, I just don't understand this math thing." Math and I have had a tumultuous relationship ever since. I didn't want to touch it with a ten-foot pole. I sat in the back of the class and disengaged. It wasn't worth the effort if I clearly lacked the talent, right?

In the documentary *She Started It*, (directed & produced by Nora Poggi and Insiyah Saeed) the narrator notes that this occurrence happens on a gendered basis. When a female receives a poor grade in a STEM subject, she is more likely to internalize it: "This means I'm bad at this." On the flip side, when a male receives a poor grade in a STEM subject, he is more likely to externalize it - blaming the class or the teacher - and is more willing to try again. (Note: this can be true, even beyond STEM. Some people internalize - assume it's their fault - any time something doesn't jive. Miscommunication and mishaps are a part of life. No need to internalize or blame. Try again!)

Some teachers, even with the best intentions, are subconsciously disposed to call on boys for the answers in math class. Perhaps they assume the boys know the correct answer. Perhaps they're sparing those who may not. Perhaps more boys raise their hands. Whatever the case, it could be contributing to the cycle of internalization and perpetuating the stereotype that males are better than females at math.

My friend's eight-year-old daughter, who loves math, refuses to join her school's math club because she doesn't want to be the only girl in the club, and doesn't want to be judged for being a girl who not only likes, but is good at, math. As parents, sisters, friends, we should encourage the girls and women in our lives to disregard outdated judgments and stereotypes and move toward their natural inclinations and curiosities.

A mere 18% of all Computer Science graduates are

female. Chances are, if you take a math or science class by choice or because it's your major, you'll find the lecture hall filled disproportionately with men. If you're inclined to these studies, kudos! You're part of an elite group! Take advantage. There may be increased opportunities for women in these fields. Women are breaking through the ceiling in EVERY area. But encouragement and support is critical. Connect with other women who've had success in your field. Connect with your female peers. The power of women coming together is the most magical power of all! With an army of women supporting you, there are truly no limits.

I had to take a math class in college, and Quantitative Reasoning proved to be quite the challenge. I had to work really hard and fight the frustration. "Why don't I get this?" I didn't understand. I continuously told my professor I was just "bad at math", so he wouldn't be surprised after grading the first test. I didn't know he was frustrated every time I said that until he gave us a pep talk on the final day of class. "I cannot stand it when ANY of you say you are bad at math," he started, "because NONE of you are bad at math! But if you keep believing you are, you'll keep performing in line with that." He recognized that a negative track record in a particular subject can perpetuate the aversion or fear, and ultimately performance. He wanted to empower everyone in the class. With those few words, the professor began to shift how we all viewed ourselves and the narrative we'd been playing.

Not long after, I decided to take a coding class because it, well... terrified me. I don't know what your self-beliefs are, but mine were very anti-coding. No way could I do it, that's for "techies", I will probably fail. Although I knew I wanted to try, the paralyzing insecurity that I wouldn't do well lashed its fangs that first hour. I felt stuck. I felt frustrated. It seemed everyone in the room was solving the puzzles with ease, whereas I was entirely confused. I called the teacher over several times, and felt ashamed every time I raised my hand. Was everyone watching? Was I taking on an insurmountable task? I felt like I didn't belong.

The instructor offered me a different way of thinking about where I was stuck. Once I reassured myself that it was okay to not know something, I immediately felt at ease. I realized I could just have fun. This wasn't a test - this was play time. If I got stuck, I could ask another question. (Note: you can always ask questions. They don't make you look stupid. We need to ask for expertise along the way - so ask away!)

Once the pressure was off, I actually didn't have questions. Suddenly, with a simple change in mindset, I was plowing through the lessons. I was so ahead of the rest of the class that when I finally asked a question, it was content they hadn't yet covered. Ok, I'll brag a bit: I was killing it. But the point is that I was good at it because my only goal was proving I could do it for myself. And because my relationship with myself is a loving, safe place, the experiment was fun.

STEM fields as a whole, however, remained a mystery to me until my summer job at the magazine *Innovation & Tech Today*. Despite facing my fears and tackling the coding class, I lacked much interest in STEM when I started. I presumed I could write about it regardless, because that's what I was good at. I started the column "Women Innovate!" because I'm always looking for ways to empower women. Then it dawned on me: maybe, on some level, I was doing this because I wanted to understand STEM myself. I've never liked the feeling of not being good at something. I decided the intention of the column should be demystifying the idea of women in the tech and entrepreneurship world. Somewhere in the mix of sharing their stories and reading others, I'd find inspiration for myself.

Not all of us are destined to be tech and entrepreneurship gurus. It's okay if we aren't rockstars in all areas of life. But the process of examining the uncomfortable spaces poises us for success. Learning about women in tech greatly enhanced my ability to be the best CEO I can be for my non-profit. Breaking down my limiting beliefs regarding STEM greatly enhanced my ability to perform well in those classes. While it's smart to tap into your interests and curiosities as you decide what to pursue, there is also value in facing your fears.

You were placed in this world with a unique set of talents, interests, attributes, and traits. As you go through life, experiences and circumstances tend to encourage or dissuade you from taking certain risks or applying yourself in certain ways. Chances are, the person you've become is along the lines of who you want to be. Just remember to stay open to areas you haven't pursued. You never know what gems exist for you in that space. Spend time experimenting. Have fun. Play. Even if you stumble, you're bound to take away something great. So, go. Challenge yourself. Face your fears. And be without limits.

18

She is

UNDERSTANDING FEMINISM

FEATURING REBECCA SCHNEIDER

HHS: I want to introduce a very influential woman in my life to join me on a more theoretical topic: my favorite topic, in fact. Drum roll, please... Feminism! Rebecca Schneider taught my Women in Literature course at the University of Colorado at Boulder in Spring 2015 (second semester of my freshman year). To me, she embodies brilliance. She speaks with a fervor that makes you listen with your heart. She poses questions that invoke the most critical thinking. She is truly one of the most intelligent women I have ever had the pleasure of meeting, and I am grateful for even the shortest of moments in intellectual conversation with her. This is a woman who makes me think beyond my typical limitations, and encourages her students to dig beneath the surface. Although her specialty in feminism is the British Romantic era, she uncovers the relevance to modern society in a way that traces influence and demands insightful musing.

RS: Thanks, Haley! The true joy of my intellectual life has been meeting students like you who inspire and sharpen my analytical practice. I have been so proud to watch from a distance as you take the helm of literacy and female empowerment projects like this one. To be invited to participate directly thrills me beyond words.

HHS: I wanted to speak with you about feminism in a unique way. It has occurred to me that feminism has suffered from a too narrow interpretation — "man hating", of course, comes to mind as the most grossly misunderstood interpretation. The diverse and contradicting interpretations of the feminist agenda stagnates the movement. Straightening the record to merely state the true, yet simple, "feminism is equality" does not suffice. Feminism goes deeper — into the layers of our deeply held beliefs about ourselves, our capabilities, and how they contribute to our relationship with contemporary culture. Thinking critically about feminism enables us to make the limitations on gender visible. And once they are visible, we have greater tact in maneuvering through them and eliminating them.

RS: Exactly. In the same way that feminism is all about empowering *everyone* by working to create equal opportunities for all people, feminism as it relates specifically to women is about encouraging our sisters to follow the life path that resonates with them. It should not be about perpetuating stereotypes of what makes someone powerful or weak. Feminism works towards a world in which living passionately, whatever that looks like, is considered powerful.

HHS: I love that you mention this encouragement to follow what *resonates*. To encourage that in another woman is to say, "I trust what's within you, and it will not lead you astray -

it is time that you trust what's within you, too." What's critical here is the juncture of this intuitive revelation and the will to pursue it. When we encourage pursuit, what resonates in other women (and ourselves) is also a push toward (what is often perceived as) a more masculine approach. I interpret this as an acknowledgement of our innate value, and our concomitant ability to pursue what resonates. How do you think this intersection of self-agency and intuition are experienced?

RS: I think that intuition too often takes a back seat to other processes of personal agency self-empowerment. But first let me break it down even further: the concept of intuition itself is gendered. Intuition tends to be viewed as an opposite to rational, empirical, objective, and hard, factual ways of knowing. Intuition tends to be seen as soft, subtle, and *weaker*. And when we begin dividing ways of knowing into soft, subtle, and weak on the one hand and objective, hard, and strong on the other we notice the gendered connotations that apply to these ways of knowing and experiencing our world. Women face two competing narratives. On the one hand, we *are* told to trust our intuition in private or personal matters. On the other hand, when it comes to wielding power or displaying agency in public settings, we often are told that intuition is not good enough as a source of empowerment. In the public settings of our empowerment we are told to display confidence, logic, reasoning, composure — in short, masculine qualities. When I think about the role feminism plays in my own life, lately it has been all about trusting my intuition more than ever as I pursue empowerment in two very public settings: teaching and academic research. Broadly speaking, my feminism causes me to take issue with the limits of the very vocabulary we use to think through our own self-empowerment.

HHS: Particularly, intuition as a feminine quality is devalued in comparison to the masculine acquisition of knowledge, which is outward, aggressive, and concrete. I must specify that anyone can "do knowledge" in a masculine OR feminine way. The concern is that if we commit to intuition, we are giving up the masculine and its concomitant success, recognition, power. Intuition is intrinsically feminine and therefore perceived in society as weaker, as you mention. Our unnecessarily limited concepts of feminine identity or agency are not just problematic for us. We have been disposed to continue in the pursuit of hard and verifiable knowledge, rather than listening to the form of knowledge that is within us.

RS: Right! We are simply *human* at our core but exist in this world where, whether we are aware of it or not, our actions live in these coded realms. We might limit ourselves, perhaps on a subconscious level, to a specific realm of what seems to be appropriate actions based on our sense of identity. (Masculine and feminine are only two such categories which contribute to an individual's identity and expression.) My politics here are not breaking down whether an action is feminine, masculine, or whatever. But I would like to emphasize how the way in which actions become coded do have an impact on what we view as right or appropriate actions *for us personally*. For example, if someone feels she "could never run for public office", I advocate reassessing whether that sentiment comes from an internalized and unnecessarily limited concept of feminine identity or agency.

HHS: And not just indicative of something unique to us. It's hard to define what is unique to us as individuals when gender connotations are polarizing and limit our perception of our identity. Although our culture is shifting to a more "gender fluid" mentality, and is now more accepting of gender expressions on a spectrum, these masculine and feminine connotations remain and extend to virtually every aspect of our existence. It extends beyond how we appear to others. It extends to our relationship with ourselves. Even when a person discloses their intention to follow their intuition, we might see a degree of hesitancy: "This is just my intuition; I don't know for sure, but I am willing to trust myself." Compare that apologetic femininity to a masculine mentality, which is aggressive in respects to its self-righteous nature. Knowledge is absolute, whereas intuition has some wiggle room. Knowledge prevails, whereas intuition cannot be proven. How can we sit in this space and allow it to suffice?

RS: That is an important question, Haley. When we call one way of knowing "stronger" than another we privilege that way of knowing. (Because, in our culture, "stronger" means "better.") Not only is intuition perceived as weaker than so-called rational knowledge, it is perceived as less reliable, less accountable, and something to be suspicious of. Because of this bias, some people might feel that intuition is all well and good when it just so happens to point to a right choice, but are reluctant to let intuition lead. Feminism provides the foundation from which we might critique unnecessary hierarchies such as these.

HHS: Feminism provides the foundation for us to become more aware of the way these hierarchies affect our relationship with ourselves. How we view our own capabilities sets the tone for our relationship with the outer world. What value can we give if we only halfway trust what is inside of us?

RS: Brilliant! As far as your question goes, it has been at the front of my mind these past months. As a scholar, a daughter, a teacher, a sister, a mentor, a partner, and a friend, I think I've been paying a lot of attention to *how* I know that I'm making the right moves. Without this period of self-reflection, I don't know if I would have realized the strength of my own intuition nor would I have likely been championing intuition in our conversation today. Self-reflection seems key somehow, but other than that I unfortunately do not have a formula or step-by-step process to suggest.

HHS: That's fair. Intuition is not something that can be referred to in print within a textbook. It is not the cold and calculating facts. It is something warmer, deeper, and inexplicable in a verbal sense. If you've ever heard someone say, "I just know", or even felt your own heart clamor with dis-ease or invigoration, you know that intuition is rooted in feeling. It is very much in the heart space, rather than the head space. The very nature of its existence relies on its inability to be proven. The question then, is how do we hold true to how we feel, when even the act of feeling is feminine and therefore weak? How do we empower feeling to its full potential? How do we encourage other women to do the same? It is a matter of empowering other women to trust themselves and realize their innate capabilities as women. We, too, can memorize and recite the words of a textbook, but we have something to offer that extends beyond.

RS: What a revolutionary concept. But seriously, the deeper I explore in my own field of literary and cultural studies I value the innovations in method even as I gain a more complete understanding and appreciation for the tried and true path to knowledge.

HHS: Let's throw it back. The first essay I wrote for your class was about the notion of "pink pirates", (in Caren Irr's book *Pink Pirates*) which I loved so much and went on to refer to in every ensuing essay. The "pink" of Irr's title automatically *ding, ding, ding*s of the stereotypically feminine.

RS: Which Irr contrasts with the blue (think stereotypically masculine) world of copyright, ownership, and traditional ideas of property and patrilineality.

HHS: On the one hand, the pink feminine refers to the positive notions of collective ownership and the *shared* workload. On the other hand, we have the negative notion of pirates, whom are notorious for *stealing*. It seems that we are stuck in a dichotomy, and the Pink Pirate is a way for us to sit within these polarities and be comfortable in this space.

RS: The productive tension you've identified within the term "pink pirate" illustrates our earlier point about power and weakness. We owe it to ourselves to think critically about the connotations our actions have in the world — how these actions may be considered (masculine) strong according to one rubric and (feminine) weak according to another rubric. Pirates have a reputation for disrupting protocols of ownership and historically masculine flows of property. You and I likely will never see a world in which ownership and property will be reimagined in truly collective ways. Likewise, we may never see a world in which intuition is considered a formidable source of self-empowerment equal to fact-based knowledge. While recognizing that in the society we live in intuition often is considered as weak, we can still choose to trust our choice.

HHS: The main impediment between the "pink" and the "pirate" is the progression of a woman trusting her own identity. Once the "pink" meets the "pirate", a woman can disrupt the gender stereotypes by confidently standing in the middle of the binary, willing to build a community of empowerment, encouraging others to do the same. So, let's think about this from the perspective of creating our individual identity, regardless of the confines of polarized gender identities.

The way I see the modern pink pirate is someone who has the *self-agency* to trust their *intuition* and listen to what *resonates*.

The modern pink pirate is a girl without limits.

AFTERWORD

Now that we know each other a little better - and, hopefully, you know *yourself* a little better, I hope it's become crystal clear just how limitless you really are.

At the end of the *Wizard of Oz*, Dorothy is told she always had the power to go home -- it was inside of her all along. Likewise, you have gained no more power by reading this book. You have, rather, come home - to recognize the truly awe-some power within you. It's been there, whether you click your ruby red heels together, wish on a shooting star, capture a firefly and believe it is Tinkerbell, or simply look into your own eyes, in your own reflection, and say "*I am*."

It is there, in your breath, your very being -- always has been, always will be.

You are a girl without limits.

THE *She Is* WITHOUT LIMITS MANTRA

SHE IS empowered to understand her innate worth.
SHE IS empowered to rely on herself before she relies on others.
When she hears of an injustice,
   SHE IS empowered to do something about it.
SHE IS empowered to know that her hands have great influence.
She can mold, push, pull -
   SHE IS empowered to use her power for massive change, and not for ill.
SHE IS empowered to use her voice, even when it wavers.
SHE IS empowered to be wholly herself, without apologies.
SHE IS empowered to sit with the dark, but know when to turn on the light.
SHE IS empowered to hold her own hand.
SHE IS empowered to push herself to the limits.
The physical edge, emotional edge, energetic edge -
   SHE IS empowered to know when to stop.
SHE IS empowered to know when to rest.
SHE IS empowered to embrace herself in the most intimate ways possible -
   commit compassion to childhood wounds, intend to discern herself in new ways.
SHE IS empowered to embrace the painful times with the same enthusiasm she
has when she embraces the good times -
   for she knows this too shall pass, for she knows the great amount of growth in
   each phase.
SHE IS empowered to take on bigger-than-big dreams.
SHE IS empowered to believe in her capabilities.
Although she will never fully comprehend the depth of her capacity -
   she is empowered to push on further.
SHE IS empowered to define herself -
   a definition absent of her past, her scars, her failures -
   a definition that is bursting with her potential and what makes her come to life.
SHE IS empowered to take the pen and write her own story.
SHE IS empowered to claim this one life and make it everything she's ever
dreamed.
SHE IS empowered to be who she is.
SHE IS empowered to know, *she is.*
SHE IS invincible,
SHE IS bursting with love,
SHE IS authentic,
SHE IS powerful,
SHE IS EMPOWERED.

She is without limits.

Made in the USA
Coppell, TX
17 August 2020